HIT HARD!
THROW HARD!

HIT HARD!
THROW HARD!

The Secrets of Power Baseball

by Robert Smith

Illustrated by Walt Fournier

BOSTON   Little, Brown and Company   TORONTO

To Leo with love

FIRST EDITION

T 09/77

Library of Congress Cataloging in Publication Data

Smith, Robert, 1905-
  Hit hard! Throw hard!

  SUMMARY: Emphasizes the idea that baseball is for
fun and presents tips for more effective fielding,
pitching, catching, and batting.
    1. Baseball—Juvenile literature. [1. Baseball]
I. Title.
GV867.5.S62   796.357′2   77-3220
ISBN 0-316-80154-2

*Published simultaneously in Canada
by Little, Brown & Company (Canada) Limited*

PRINTED IN THE UNITED STATES OF AMERICA

CONTENTS

HIT HARD!
THROW HARD!

BASEBALL IS FOR FUN

The most important thing to remember about baseball is that it's a game. And games are for fun. Baseball is not for making your town or school Number One in the state or nation. It is not for getting even with enemies, for seeing your name in headlines, or for being interviewed on TV. It is for enjoyment. And the best part of baseball is that losers can enjoy it as much as winners, if they play the game with all their hearts. I know when I talk to former stars like Mickey Mantle, Willie Mays, Elston Howard, or Frank Crosetti that they often enjoy recalling certain great plays they made — and even when I look back on my own less than mediocre career, I like to think about a long hit I made, or an over-the-shoulder catch, or some lucky stop of a ground ball — and often we cannot recall if our side won or lost that particular game.

There are, of course, people in and around the professional game who still preach that "winning is everything" and that "nice guys finish last," but that is nonsense. Winning is a thrill, and the *desire* to win adds speed to your feet and strength to your muscles. But losing is not a tragedy. And many nice guys win championships.

If you could visit Cooperstown, New York, the site of the National Baseball Hall of Fame, on a day when the old-time stars were all in town, you would discover that most of the greatest players of the past were pleasant, agreeable, friendly, well bred, and decidedly "nice." Stanley Coveleskie, one of Cleveland's greatest pitchers, who won far more often than he lost, has always been a man who likes to laugh and tell good stories, who makes friends easily, never raises his voice, and never hurt a soul. As for Babe Ruth, the greatest ballplayer who ever lived, men who played with him will tell you: *"Nobody disliked Babe Ruth!"* He was a roughneck. But he was often generous and kind, particularly to children and people in trouble. Waite Hoyt, once a great pitcher for the greatest New York teams, is a thorough gentleman — well read, well spoken, and invariably courteous — and has been all his life, even though he put his whole soul into winning ball games. As for Leo Durocher, the man who is supposed to have invented the phrase "nice guys finish last," he played for some of the losingest ball clubs in history, brought his club in last many more times than once, and was known when he was with the New York Yankees as "the All-American Out" — yet he will admit he got great fun out of baseball from the time he was a kid.

Granting then that baseball was invented for everyone to enjoy, let's see where the fun lies.

THROW HARD!

From the earliest days, and in its most primitive forms, baseball has been a game of hitting and throwing. And it is plain that people have always played it because it is fun to hit a ball hard and to throw it with all your might.

Throwing comes first, because that is easiest. Even tiny children can throw, and they sometimes drive their poor mothers to distraction by throwing toys and eating utensils around the room. But throwing a ball is the most fun, because a ball is made to throw, being round, easy to take hold of, and inclined to travel in a fairly straight line. Stones are great fun to throw, too; Eddie Plank, the famous Philadelphia pitcher of many years ago, developed his arm by throwing them. Honus Wagner, Hall of Fame shortstop from Pittsburgh, threw lumps of coal. Bob Turley, once a fireball pitcher with the Yankees and a pitching coach with the Red Sox and the Braves, used to throw green pears in his backyard. But they all threw at *targets*. Eddie Plank used to try to knock birds off a fence. Honus Wagner threw at knotholes. Bob Turley put targets on trees and threw at them. And you too should *always* throw at a target. But you should throw *hard* at the target, not just trying to hit it but trying to hit it hard. In fact, missing the target should not worry you. Keep your eye on it. Keep throwing hard. And gradually your muscles will make the adjustment.

Before you start throwing hard, however, make sure your arm is properly warmed up, that the blood is circulating through the muscles and the muscles are loose. You can manage that by ten or twelve easy throws using only a small part of your strength. Then you can begin to throw a little harder each time until you are ready to let go with all your strength.

You should also take care to *stop throwing* the moment you feel any strain. One of the worst things you can do — and something that may finish you as a ballplayer — is to throw when the effort hurts your arm, particularly your elbow. If you just have a little cramp or stiffness in your muscles when you begin, you can usually work that out by throwing *very* easily for a few minutes. But don't throw hard until the discomfort is gone.

It is true that many great professional pitchers had to pitch when their arms hurt. But they did so knowingly, aware that they were shortening their careers but willing to do so for the sake of the high salary or the big prize that lay ahead. Don't *you* do that, even if some wild-eyed fan or eager teammate urges you to keep trying. When your arm hurts after you have been throwing hard for a while, that's your muscle telling you "ENOUGH!" Better pay heed if you want to keep on getting fun out of baseball.

This does not mean, however, that you should baby your arm by never throwing hard and by never getting tired. You should make it a habit *always* to throw (after proper warm-up) with the full length and full strength of your arm.

A proper throw begins with a reach back. Get the elbow well away from the body and, if you are right-handed, get your left foot forward, with your weight on your right foot (just the other way around if you are left-handed). Put your hand well back — as if you were reaching back to pick the ball off a table about knee

high — as far as you can reach behind you. You will notice that to "pick up" the ball, you have to cock your wrist. That will add spin and speed to your throw. As you throw, your elbow may be slightly bent on the

forward motion, but it should straighten out as your arm comes down; you should release the ball when the arm is *fully* extended. In short, you do not snap it off with the elbow held close to the body, but sling it with the full length of your arm.

The most natural motion, the one that tires the arm hardly at all, is, oddly enough, an underhand motion, like a toss. A few great pitchers have actually used this motion all through their careers, and when the game of baseball was very young the "square pitch," or toss, was actually required by the rules. But it takes a real throw to get proper speed and full distance. And so all distance throwing is done overhand, or almost overhand. The best throw is probably three-quarters overhand. Full overhand, in which the arm is brought around close to the ear, puts an unnatural strain on the arm, as you will observe when you try it. You will feel the muscles pull in both shoulder and back. It is true that many great

pitchers have "come over the top" this way, to get extra power on their pitches and a bigger break on the curve. (Taking more room to "pull down" on a curve gives it more spin.)

It is worth noting, however, that the man generally acknowledged to have been the fastest pitcher in professional baseball, Walter Johnson, threw all his pitches sidearm, as if he were picking the ball off a table not directly behind him, but around on his other side. When he threw, his arm, fully extended, acted like a slingshot. And the ball, when he let go of it, seemed to be coming directly at any right-handed batter, so that many a batter instinctively jumped away. Yet Johnson never tried to hit or even "brush back" a batter. He knew his speed was fearsome enough to do real damage if it struck a man.

The slight crooking of the elbow, as the arm is brought forward, is used to impart accuracy to any throw. It is somewhat harder to sling a ball by simple centrifugal force and have it strike the target consistently. But actually *aiming* the ball, as you would aim a dart in a dart game for instance, should be avoided. Get the arm well back and throw it with your full arm. Practice and practice and more practice will bring accuracy.

There is real pleasure in firing a ball this way, full strength, as long as your arm is well readied. Even if you have no ambition to be a pitcher, you will get a great deal of satisfaction from seeing how far you can throw a ball and with what impact you can strike the target. It is best if you have someone to throw to, to provide a target with a glove. But even if you are by yourself and have only apples to throw, or a tennis ball, you can still get a kick out of banging a target. You can set soda cans up on a fence and try to knock them off. Or you can simply mark a target somewhere and try to hit it good and hard — hard enough to make a noise. (Cy Young's catcher, during this Hall of Famer's warm-up throws, used to stand aside now and then and let a ball hit the fence, to scare the opponents with the thunderous crack it made.)

Don't fret too much about accuracy at the start. Work on it by always keeping your eye on the spot you want to hit. But don't start easing up to see how close you can come to the bull's-eye. Keep banging away full strength. It's more fun and it will make the game more fun when you start to play it, because you will be able to get the ball to the target *fast*. It may take a long time before your throws start to come into the circle. But never mind. Fire away! Have fun!

A few coaches will still ridicule a player by telling him he "throws like a girl," as if girls were physically incapable of throwing properly. But nowadays most people know that's nonsense. Girls years ago threw badly because they had never been allowed to play ball games, or had been discouraged from playing "boys' games" of any sort. So they threw just as most people do who have never learned how to fire a ball properly — with the wrong foot forward, usually, and with the elbow in front of their bodies. Once anyone, male or female, learns the trick of getting the arm behind the body on the throw, the ball will start to travel hard and fast.

Some young people with ambitions to pitch start right away to think about throwing curves and trick pitches of every sort, and often they keep asking to be shown how a screwball is thrown, or a knuckleball, a slider, or a sharp curve.

Well, a curve is simple enough. But it is not necessary right away. And trick pitches will hamper the development of your throwing strength. As a matter of fact, when a professional baseball scout wants to say a good word about a young pitcher, he will say simply: "He throws hard!" That's what really counts — throwing hard. And next in importance is the ability to hit a target, to put your pitches where you want them to go. With speed and control, you can build a whole career of pitching. The other pitches are all "extras," and you can develop them when you have brought your arm to its full strength and have learned how to put every pitch where you want it.

Using the *full length* and the *full strength* of your arm — that is what develops unusual pitching or throwing ability. As for control, that does not come from trying to steer the ball on its way, easing up so as to *push* the ball to the target. It comes from throwing hard at a target often enough so that you learn how to hit it. It would seem obvious therefore that speed comes first. It may seem a contradiction to say that you should throw at a target and that you should not worry about missing it, but that is what you should do all the same. Get your eye on the target as you throw. Throw hard. And eventually — after fifteen throws, or fifty throws, or a hundred throws — your eye and muscles will begin to coordinate properly and you will start coming closer and closer until finally you are able to hit it nearly every time.

Here is another habit you should form right away: always step when you throw. If you are a right-hander, complete a throw with your right foot as the pivot foot, then shove off with that foot as you let the ball go. If you don't do this, if you throw entirely with your arm, you are almost sure to develop a sore arm eventually. And you will not be getting your full strength into your throw. Later on, when you are actually playing the game, there may be times when you have to snap off a throw without a step. But that will be the rare exception.

Finally, you should follow through. Don't leave your hand pointing at the target. Bring the arm right down across the body so that your throwing hand winds up by

the opposite hip. Just watch any good pitcher or out-fielder in action and you will see what the follow-through looks like. A good follow-through, making one smooth, complete motion of the throw, will take strain off your elbow and give added power to your throw.

As for practice, you can really get that almost any-where. You don't even need a baseball or a glove, or a base, or someone to catch your throws or coach you. You can put a mark on a fence or a brick wall and use a ball that will bounce back — a rubber ball or a tennis ball. If you are lucky enough to live near a beach of some kind, you probably can gather up a lot of stones, then toss a chip of wood out into the water for a target or aim at a distant rock. Start with easy throws, just slow-motion stuff to get the blood circulating in your muscles and work any little stiffness out of your arm. Speed up gradually. Then throw *hard!* Keep banging at that target. Or use the last splash you made for a target and see if you can land your throw there again. If the target is too close, pick one a little farther out and try to reach it. Throw until you sweat. Or until a twinge in your arm tells you it is time to quit. Just be very sure you *do* quit when you feel a twinge of any sort. Perhaps you are not throwing properly. Perhaps you are trying so hard to hit the target you are forgetting to follow through. Perhaps you need to quit throwing for a day or two, until the arm is completely comfortable again.

Now let's see what kind of throws you have to make in order to play the different positions on the baseball diamond.

The Pitcher

As a rule, most people, when they first begin to play baseball, want to pitch. That's because the pitcher is one of two players who are playing the game all the time. (The catcher does too.) He sets the pace of the game and he has the most fun. Or it seems that way to anyone watching. When Ted Williams started to play baseball, he was a pitcher. So was Babe Ruth. And Mickey Mantle pitched in high school. Babe became the best pitcher in the American League. Ted became the greatest hitter. But Ted pitched in the big leagues too. In 1940, Ted pitched two innings for the Boston Red

Sox, struck out one batter, gave up three hits, and allowed one run. Mickey Mantle used to win Cokes from his teammates by fooling them with his knuckleball.

Pitching differs from throwing in that the pitcher is, or should be, far more concerned with the placement of his throws, the variations in their speed, and the deceptiveness of his delivery. He has to keep the batter from seeing the ball too soon (that's why he sometimes hides it behind his leg) and prevent the batter from timing the arrival of the ball too easily. So he has to put in a lot of practice at keeping the batter guessing. He does this by schooling himself to make all his preliminary motions look alike, regardless of what sort of pitch he is going to throw, and by taking care to release the ball at about the same point in his motion.

But before he goes in for refinements like that, he has to learn to throw hard and to throw accurately. A pitcher, once he has strengthened his arm sufficiently by a lot of hard throwing, should always practice with a catcher and something to mark off the area of the plate over which he is going to throw. Of course, practicing on a regular diamond is ideal. But it's simple enough to mark out an imaginary plate in the dirt, or to set a bit of plank down to indicate the proper width (17 inches). It's the width of the plate that matters in determining the strike zone.

After the proper warm-up of a dozen or more easy throws, back and forth, you can start to throw hard. But, as a pitcher, you are limited by the rules as to just what moves you can make in delivering the ball to the plate, and you might as well start at once to get used to these limitations. First of all, you must stay in contact with the "rubber," which is the plate from which the pitcher works. You need not stand right on it. In fact, it is better if you don't. But, to keep you from sneaking up closer and closer to the batter and letting the ball go right in his face, you have to keep one foot touching the rubber until you let the ball go. The foot that holds contact is the pivot foot. For a right-hander, the pivot foot is the right foot; for a left-hander, the left.

You can make a mark in the dirt to represent the rubber, if you like, and work from that. As you prepare to pitch, your pivot foot will be on the rubber, with the toe pointed toward the plate, and the other foot behind (this is the nobody-on base position). On starting your motion, you lift the pivot foot and set it down right in

front of the rubber, in contact with it and parallel to it. This is so you can get a good *shove* off the rubber as you deliver the ball.

Frank Crosetti, the famous New York Yankee coach, used to complain that many young pitchers, even in the major leagues, "pitched too quick." By that he did not mean that they were throwing the ball too hard and fast, but rather that they were pitching too soon, too early in their motion. Instead of reaching back and getting the entire weight of their bodies on the pivot foot, they were starting to release the ball with much of their weight actually in front of the rubber, on the free foot, so that they were not making use of their full strength. This sort of pitching tires the pitcher quickly and makes for sore arms. To avoid this, you should always reach back to that imaginary table for the ball. As you do, you will be striding forward with your free foot — the one that is not in contact with the rubber. This rocking motion will get all your weight solidly on your pivot foot, so that when you shove forward to pitch you will be throwing all your weight as well as your strength behind the ball. Your free foot will come down first and, ideally, you will bring your pivot foot up parallel with it as you let go

of the ball. But you must be sure to *bend your knees*, so that you do not land stiff-legged. A few good pitchers never learned to bend their knees as they landed, so they actually fell off the mound on completion of the pitch. Jim Bunning, who pitched no-hit games in both leagues, never did cure himself of this stiff-legged habit and as a result he was often down on his hands and knees beside the mound after a pitch, unable to field a bunt. Fortunately he had so much talent that he could afford this very bad fault. But you'll do a lot better if you avoid it.

The use of the feet and legs is most important to a pitcher. The long stride with the free foot (left foot in a right-hander) helps provide the speed to your fast ball. And the shove off the rubber with your pivot foot provides that last bit of *oomph* that gives the ball extra velocity.

A big strong pitcher who relies on his speed to overpower a batter will usually take an extra long stride as he delivers the ball. Because of that, he may have to land flat-footed. But until you develop into a power pitcher, it is best to try to land on your toes as you make your forward stride. And the bent knees will help you retain your balance.

Most people who develop sore arms in baseball are pitchers, or try to be pitchers. So it is especially important, if you want to keep on enjoying the game and like to pitch, that you take care not to overdo while your muscles are still developing. What spoils most young pitching arms is the pressure to keep on throwing when the arm hurts — the desire to throw to just one more batter, to win this game at all costs. That attitude may be all right when you are fully grown and well muscled. But when you are just starting, it can put a quick end to a pitching career and take all the fun out of the game.

A smart pitcher never abuses his arm anyway. Pros often pitch in pain and you may even run into amateur coaches who will tell you that that is what you must do to develop into a big leaguer. But perhaps you don't want to be a big leaguer. Perhaps you just want to make the team and keep on playing as long as you can. And even if you do nurse some desire to make baseball your profession, you are not going to advance your career by injuring your arm. So when your arm hurts, stop pitching. Usually the pain will come at the elbow joint, but sometimes, especially if you are not getting your full body into the pitch, or are striding unnaturally to favor a sore foot or to adjust to uneven ground, you will get pain in the shoulder. At the first twinge it's time to quit. You may be able to start tossing the ball in an easy manner the next day. But don't throw hard again until it stops hurting.

One good way to ease strain on your arm is by using a generous windup. The windup is not used just to fool the batter. It helps you establish a good natural rhythm that will distribute the effort of the pitch through all your muscles and put no undue strain on any one. Most

good windups begin with a forward movement as the ball
is lifted up about head-high and the bare hand and
glove hand are brought together. This is done as you
move your pivot foot to set it parallel to the rubber. Some
pitchers even lift the ball well above their heads while
they make this move. But you do what comes to you

most easily and naturally. Swing your arms forward. Bring the hands together. Then, as you are making your forward stride, reach *way* back to pick that ball off the imaginary table behind you. Try to make it into one easy motion. Don't stride out too far. Don't stop in the middle of the windup to cock your arm or adjust your grip on the ball. The vital part of the motion is that backward and forward sweep as you lift your leg, stride forward, reach back, and throw. Make the throw a part of that motion. Don't just tack it on at the end.

When you have found — by adjusting the length of your stride, the backward reach, the lifting of the front foot — the motion that comes easiest to you, stick with it and work on it all the time. Eventually, you may want to add some little frills to it — movements of the head, flips with the glove, hunch of a shoulder — to keep the batter off balance. But those are tricks you can work on only *after* you have developed the smooth basic motion.

I don't believe you should start early in your career to concern yourself with trick pitches of any kind. If you can put your pitches where you want them to go, you won't need any fancy pitches to get batters out. But there is a good deal of fun in fooling a batter with a change of pace — and you can master that pitch without going in for any fancy methods of snapping the wrist or twisting the arm in the wrong direction (as you do when throwing a screwball, for instance).

If you have a good smooth motion, you can soon learn to deliver an off-speed pitch with a motion that looks (to the batter) exactly like the one you use for your fast ball. The natural and best way to hold the ball when you throw hard is with the first two fingers on top of the ball and the thumb underneath. You squeeze the ball tight between the first joints of your fingers on top and the first joint of your thumb underneath. This tight grip imparts the spin that gives the ball extra speed and may even cause it to veer off a straight line — to "hop" as they say.

But to throw a half-speed pitch, you hold the ball a

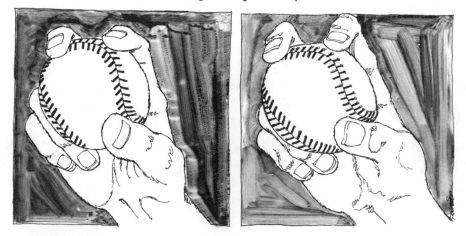

little bit deeper in your hand. And as you let it go, you lift the first joints of fingers and thumb right off the ball, so it develops very little spin. It just slips out of the loose grip and floats toward the batter. And because you have gone through your regular pitching motion, he will be expecting it to come at the same speed as your fast ball and, if you have been successful in deceiving him, he will step into the pitch and start his swing long before the ball gets there.

It really is fun to see a batter try to catch his balance and then flail feebly at a ball that has fooled him. But you have to remember that if you don't have a fast pitch that you can control, the off-speed pitch, or change-up, is not going to help you.

In delivering the change-up, you will not of course shove off from the rubber with the effort you use in throwing the fast ball. As a matter of fact, while you are working to get control of this pitch (and it does take a lot of practice to make it come into the strike zone) you can let your pivot foot stay in contact with the rubber as you complete your motion. Or just drag it slowly along to bring the foot up parallel with your front foot. After you know you can control the pitch, you can start *lifting* your pivot foot off the rubber and bringing it up, so you complete the whole motion, fast-ball style.

Now on this matter of control: You can begin to concern yourself with that once you are satisfied with your motion in delivering the ball. You should concern yourself first with the up-and-down control. That is, do not worry about the width of the plate or about the width of the strike zone. Think first about getting that ball *low*. Pick out your target on the legs of the guy you are throwing to. Take a spot just above his knee and tell yourself you are going to hit that. Then bang at it with all your might. And keep throwing at it until he regularly begins to catch the ball reasonably close to the spot you picked out.

A pitcher who can keep the ball below the batter's waist whenever he wants to is going to have himself a lot of fun seeing that guy swing over the ball, or top it so that it bounces along the ground. (There are hitters who do well with low pitches. But you will find that they don't grow very thick in your neighborhood.) Of course once you have this up-and-down control, you can come in with a high pitch now and then so the batter can't count on finding the ball in the same spot all the time.

And when you have the up-and-down control, you will find the inside-outside control follows easily.

A simple curve is a good pitch to have, although it is not an absolute essential. Some of the best fast-ball pitchers had only a modest curve ball and used it almost entirely as a "waste" pitch — a pitch thrown well out of the strike zone, just to keep the batter from timing the fast ball too easily.

A curve is often used as a change-up too. It differs from a fast ball in the way it is thrown and the way it is released. But it can be thrown with the same basic motion, with a slight difference in the forward stride and a change in the way the hand is held. To get the right sort of spin on a curve ball you need more "air" in which to pull down on the ball. So you shorten your stride just enough to permit your arm, as it sweeps in its forward arc, to reach a few inches higher than it would with the fast ball. You do not need to concentrate on getting the hand up higher. Just make your forward stride a bit shorter and your hand, as it comes over the top, will naturally reach a higher point at the top of the arc.

As you complete the motion, turn your hand over, so as to release the ball, not from the tips of fingers and

thumb but from the crotch between thumb and fore-finger, so the ball rolls off the side of the index finger. The spin thus provided impels the ball to turn in a sideways manner that will cause it to move away from a right-handed batter (if you throw right-handed). Pitchers who depend on sharp curves to get batters out impart extra spin to the ball in releasing it by giving an extra sharp snap to the forearm and wrist. But this is not advised when you are trying to develop your throwing arm. Wait until you get your full strength and full growth before you start doing tricks with your arm. Control and speed are far more effective than dipsy-doodling. A nice slow curve that just dips out of the strike zone is a great change-up from a good fast ball and it will send most amateur batters fishing. And believe me, that's fun too — to see a batter nearly break his back to reach WAY out over the plate to hit a ball that is just tantalizingly out of reach. Of course if you don't have that good fast ball to set him up for the curve, he'll probably wait long enough to see what the ball is going to do and so won't reach for it.

Come to think of it, the reason pitchers have the most fun of any ballplayer is that they have so many things they can do on a ball diamond, so many problems to solve, so many different ways of getting batters out. They can size up a batter by the way he stands at the plate or by the way he works in batting practice, then plan their strategy accordingly. If a batter stands well away from the plate, he can be "set up" with an inside pitch that does not go over the plate, then he can often be fooled with a good low outside fast ball that cuts the edge of the strike zone. If a batter has an open stance, with his forward foot pointing off toward one of the basemen rather than at the pitcher, he is probably looking for an inside pitch, or at least is ready for such a pitch. So if you offer him anything inside, make sure it is out of the strike zone, where he cannot get a good wallop at it.

Unless you are blessed with a mighty pair of shoulders and so have a fiery fast ball that you can throw all day without tiring, don't try to strike all the batters out. Your basic strategy should be to get ahead of the batter in the count, getting more strikes on him than balls, so he will have to hit the pitch you want him to hit — a good low pitch, perhaps, that he will most likely bounce to an infielder for an easy out.

Batters who hold the bat down at the knob and swing the full length of the bat, turning completely around in a follow-through, are the ones who are trying for distance all the time. They like fast balls and can sometimes be set up for a change of pace. Or, if there are men on base with two out and their club desperately needing runs, they may even swing at a pitch thrown so low it will almost bounce at their feet.

But when a batter is eager to hit, and a hit is going to put his club ahead, you do not want to make the mistake of trying to tease him with a trick off-speed pitch right in the strike zone. When you feel sure he is going to swing, put your pitch where he is not going to get a good piece of it. Bill Lee made this mistake in the 1975 World Series when he tossed up a lollipop pitch that floated through the strike zone. He just *knew* the batter would swing at it. Perez did and it went for a home run.

It is always good practice to go with your best pitch in a crucial situation. And the very best pitch is often a fast ball, placed where the batter cannot get his best leverage on it.

One mistake you do not want to make in choosing your strategy is to ease up on the weak hitters — the guys at the end of the batting order. Often the only pitch these batters can handle is a soft pitch, even out of the strike zone. So look for your strikeouts from these fellows. Throw hard! Bear down! Get them out of there!

You are not a complete pitcher unless you can field your position. Of course you do not want to get tangled up in infield plays that can best be handled by other fielders. But there are a number of plays in which you *must* take part. And if you fail to do so, you may cost your club a run.

Like an infielder or an outfielder, you must be ready for *every* ball to be hit back to you. That is why, in completing your motion, you bring your pivot foot up beside your leading foot and stand with knees bent, hands ready to grab the ball. And *every* time a ball is hit on the ground to your left, you must start toward first base. Many times you will be able to field the ball. If you have a good chance for it, bend your knees and bend your back and get right down to it with both hands in front of you. But don't chase a ground ball or try to round it up. If it goes past you quickly, it is going to be a chance for the first baseman or the second baseman and you may be needed to take the throw at the base. So get over there fast, with your eye on the ball, and be ready to accept the fielder's throw. Watch the ball all the time, so you will know where it is coming from and when. If it is a really bad throw, you may have to forget about the base and keep the ball from getting by.

Often you will be getting to the base about the same time as the runner. If he is close to you, *do not run across the bag!* Instead, once you have the ball in your hand securely, hit the bag with your right foot, on the second

base side, and keep right on going in the same direction as the runner. Don't risk a collision with the runner. He will be moving at desperation speed and could really damage you if he ran into you.

Bunted balls are often a pitcher's responsibility. Some pitchers have been practically driven out of the game by their inability to field bunts. So give yourself plenty of practice with these. One danger you must avoid is being nonchalant, or careless as you pick up the ball. Fielding a bunt is a *difficult* play. Even if the ball is merely trickling toward you, you cannot afford to fancy-dan it or take the out for granted. Keep your eye fixed on the ball. Don't look over to first base until *after* you have the ball in your hand. Round the ball up with your glove and grab it with your bare hand. Unless it is very slowly hit, and right along the baseline, you will have plenty of chance to throw the man out.

Once you have the ball, look to first, to make sure the bag is covered. (Sometimes the first baseman may be charging in for the bunt too.) Then, face the target — the baseman — and throw overhand, hard. Don't steer the ball. Gun it right to the fielder's glove. Avoid a sidearm or underhand throw unless you are in a desperate hurry.

Those throws have a tendency to curve or dip and may give the baseman trouble.

If the ball is on the baseline, it is usually the job of the first or third baseman to handle it. But you move toward it anyway, for if it is a short bunt, you'll have to capture it. On a bunt on the first baseline, remember to throw *inside* the line to the base. The runner is required to run outside the line and you do not want to hit him.

A good bunt on the third baseline may leave you with no play to make. If the ball is right on the line, it is best to leave it alone and hope it rolls foul. The instant it rolls into foul territory, brush it right away with your glove, so it won't roll back. But *if* you play it, be sure to take a good look at the base before you throw. And don't throw if the runner has the base made. Every extra throw makes an extra chance for an error.

Sometimes, on a sacrifice bunt, if you are able to field the ball quickly, you may have a chance to put the lead runner out at second or third. But don't worry about the runner until *after* you have the ball in your throwing hand. Then, before letting the ball fly, *look* to see if you have a play. Your teammates, and especially the catcher, will probably be shouting to you "Second!" or "Third!" but even if they do, *look first* and unless there is a chance to get the lead runner, turn back to first and get the out there. If you make a hopeless throw and lose both runners, it's your fault. Don't blame the guys who were telling you where to throw.

You will often be involved on throws from the outfield, especially those to third base or home. Third base is a real danger spot. An overthrow that gets away there almost always means a run. So you get over as fast as you can move, when there is a throw from the outfield to third, and back up the baseman. Get about twenty-five

feet behind him. (If you are too close, a bad throw can bounce past both of you!) And take a position in line with the expected throw. Watch the ball all the way — not the runner. If it gets by the third baseman, capture it in both hands and, unless there is a play at the plate, carry it back into the diamond.

The pitcher is usually the only man who can back up the catcher on a throw from the outfield, or cover the plate on a throw that gets by the catcher. Be alert to get down to the plate, if a pitch gets by when there is a runner in scoring position. But don't try to block the runner off the plate or you may wind up in the first-aid room. A runner moving full tilt into a stationary player is going to give *all* the impact to the man who is standing still. Just make sure you have a tight grip on the ball. Hold it with your bare fingers and protect it with the glove. Hold the runner off with your glove and lay the tag on him from the side as he comes in. Keep your hands low, so he cannot slide under the tag, and don't stand in there once the tag is made.

Many times, when there is a lot of room between the plate and the backstop, a ball that goes by the catcher may draw the catcher a long way behind the diamond, so he will have an extra long throw to make to keep a runner from taking extra bases. Don't forget, when this happens, even if there is no runner on third, you should get down toward the plate and make ready to relay a throw to second or third. If ball four, for instance, escapes the catcher, the ball is alive and the runner can take as many bases as he can make. But if you are on hand to shorten the throw, you can hold the runner to first base.

On pop fouls in front of the plate, or on short pop flies, you must captain the play, by shouting to indicate which player should get the ball. Ordinarily, if an infielder has a good chance to make the catch, you should call the catcher off, for an infielder's glove is easier to catch with than is the catcher's. If the catcher does not hear you or ignores you, you may have to run over and take hold of him to keep him from banging into the infielder. A catcher with his full equipment on is a pretty dangerous object to collide with. Both players, on a pop fly, may have their eyes focused on the ball and be unaware of the danger. So it will be up to you to make the rescue.

Fielding your position well is a skill you will develop

only from experience. But there are certain good habits you can develop as you play.

Number one: Keep your eye on the ball. Do not look up to check the runner or the baseman until you have the ball solidly in your grip. You can make an awful fool of yourself by reaching down for an "easy" pickup and coming up with a handful of air.

Number two: Always be ready to have the ball come back to you. Be out in front of the box, with hands in front of you and knees bent.

Number three: Do not try to field ground balls without bending your back. Bend your knees. Bend your back. Get right over the ball and watch it into your glove.

It is important for the pitcher to learn to keep runners from getting a jump on him. You should know where the runners are as you take your position on the mound and you should check to see that they are not getting too far off the bag. Of course you will not use your full windup when you have runners on base. And you will start with your pivot foot against the rubber and your free foot out front. You can loosen your arms by reaching with both hands above your head, then bring the ball down in both hands, until it is about chest-high. But you still must *reach back* to get your full weight behind the pitch. You do not however commit yourself to the pitch even then, for, if you have seen the man on first moving too far off the bag, you can, as you make your stride, stride *toward* first instead of toward the plate and fire a hard throw there. (You *must* throw, however, if you make any move toward first. You may fake throws to second, but not to first.)

To keep track of the runner on first, you do not have to look him in the eye. All you need to do is keep track of his feet. A left-hander, who will be facing first base, has no trouble with this. A right-hander can see the runner's feet if he just looks down and a little to his left as he takes his position on the mound — left foot forward, right foot in front of the rubber but in contact with it.

It is important not to get in the habit of turning to look at the runner before you pitch. Take a position that will enable you to throw either to the plate or to first without shifting your back foot. Then practice lifting your forward foot in just the same way for the throw to the plate or the throw to the bag. You will of course bring your foot down in a different place on the throw to the bag. But you don't want the runner to know too soon which way you are going to throw.

But *you* must know which way you are going. Do not start to pitch with one eye on the runner, thinking you will change direction if you see him go. Decide, as you check the runner, whether you are going to go to first base with the throw or not. Perhaps if he is getting too much of a lead off the bag, you may throw to first two or three times in a row, until you are satisfied that he has shortened his lead. Then, once you have decided to pitch, *forget the runner!* Concentrate on the hitter. If the runner goes from a short lead, you have done your part and the catcher at least has a better chance of nailing him if he goes.

In amateur baseball, a change of pace to first base often works magically. You may lob the ball at half speed over to the first baseman three or four times, until the runner has begun to trot back rather lazily to tag up. Then, starting from your pitching position, fire the ball *hard* over to the base and you may give your first baseman an easy put-out.

Once in a while, particularly in amateur baseball, a

runner may challenge you by moving far down the line toward second base. Sometimes you can get him back simply by lifting your rear foot off the rubber and setting it down behind the rubber. This frees you to throw to the bag as you please and he will probably get back. If he does not, just start directly toward him. Make him move one way or the other. (If you throw to first too soon, he may break for second, with a good chance of making it.) If he bluffs one way or the other, trying to make you throw, just run right toward him, ready to put the tag on him. If you are on the baseline and he bluffs a run right at you, *keep coming*. Don't wait for him. When he finally breaks away and sprints for the base, throw to the baseman ahead of him.

A runner on second base can be faked back to the base just by turning quickly, with the ball in your hand, and stepping off the rubber. When you have played enough ball to have confidence in your ability to throw quickly and accurately, you can even work out a pickoff play with your shortstop. This is a "count" play and will require you to practice with your shortstop so you will both be counting in the same rhythm. Then you can take your position on the mound and not look at the runner at all.

The catcher will be watching him and he will give the signal when the man is far enough off base so there is daylight showing between him and the shortstop (with the runner being farther from the base than the shortstop). The catcher will then give the agreed sign (perhaps picking up a little dirt) and you and the shortstop can immediately start counting. When you reach the agreed-on count, turn quickly and fire the ball hard to the shortstop. You should throw it so as to get to him *before* he gets to the base. This is a pretty play when it works right and can give your club a lift by rubbing out a runner who is in scoring position.

A runner on third base can be an annoyance if you let him distract you. Many runners will try hard to break the pitcher's concentration by bluffing a run for the plate as he begins his stretch. You can usually drive these guys back to the base by just looking at them. If you keep your eye on them for a few seconds, and the third baseman at the same time moves closer to the bag, the runner, if he has any sense, will duck back in a hurry. Sometimes you may have to back off the rubber (rear foot first) to get him back to the bag. But once you are satisfied that he is staying close enough to the bag, you can concentrate on the batter and pay no heed to the runner's shenanigans.

In school and amateur leagues, the suicide squeeze is an important play. This is the play in which the runner starts from third base as soon as the pitcher commits himself to the pitch. The runner goes full speed for home and the batter squares off into bunting position and tries to bunt the ball just out in front of the plate. If his bunt is successful, the run is almost sure to score.

If you take care not to forget that there is a runner on third, you may be able to break this play up rather easily. What you must *not* do is get excited and try to hurry your throw to the plate. Whatever you throw, the batter still has a right to try to hit it, so you don't want to feed him something that is easy to bunt. The best way to break up this play is to go right ahead and pitch the ball in your regular rhythm but let it fly *right at the batter.* Don't worry. It won't hit him, and you should not be trying to hit him. He will be facing you squarely in bunting stance and can easily avoid the ball. But it will be extremely difficult for him to bunt such a pitch. He will most likely just jump out of the way. If he does get his bat on the ball, it is very likely to pop off into foul territory.

But you must also move toward the plate quickly on this play, in case he does bunt the ball successfully. Chances are, unless he hits the ball harder than he should or the runner is very slow, you won't be able to stop the run if you field the ball. But you must not forget that the batter will be running too, and if there is obviously no play at the plate, you must fire the ball to first — *inside* the baseline.

There is one bit of advice all good pitchers will give you that may sound contradictory. After urging you to develop a good smooth motion, they may warn you not to make it "too smooth." All that means is that you must not get yourself into such a groove that batters will find it easy to time your pitches. This probably will be nothing to worry about in sandlot baseball, or even in school games where you do not see the same batters more than a few times a season. But it is good fun sometimes to get a batter off balance by changing your own timing just a bit. You can do that perhaps by not bringing the ball up so high as you start your windup. If you have been raising it over your head, for instance, as you bend into your windup, you may start to lift it only chin-high at the beginning. Or you may hurry up the last part of your motion, shoving off the rubber a little more quickly, so the ball starts to the plate just a split second sooner.

Pitchers have to be especially careful of their equipment. One thing most pitchers insist on is a good big glove, because sometimes a batted ball comes back like a shot and you need something to throw up in front of your face for protection. You should also take a good look at your shoes before you start, and make sure you do not have a loose spike-plate. A loose plate may catch in the rubber and throw you, or give your foot a bad twist.

Remember too that pitchers pitch with their legs as

well as their arms. That good shove and long stride are important parts of your delivery and help provide the power to your pitches. And while your arm gets plenty of workout in a game, the legs need even more than you can give them on the mound. In the big leagues, most pitchers run every day except just before and after pitching. A few will run *every* day, regardless. It may not be quite so easy for you to find opportunity and space to run if you live in the city. But you should run as often as you get the chance, and run until you are really sweating hard and are taking your breath in big gulps. When there is no chance to run, you can exercise your leg muscles by taking all steps two at a time, by bicycling, or by jumping rope. It will surprise you how much harder you will be able to throw when your leg muscles are stronger. And the harder you can throw, the more fun you are going to get out of pitching.

The Catcher

The catcher has the hardest job in baseball. He gets some of the hardest knocks, often has to catch the most fiery pitches, has to leap like a cat on bunted balls, snag towering fouls, and throw out base runners or keep them close. Besides that, he has to help plan the pitcher's strategy, call all the pitches, know all the batters' habits, keep the pitcher cool, keep the fielders on their toes and see that they are not out of position, and act as captain on many infield plays, naming the fielder to catch a ball and the base to throw to. And when the bases are empty he has to hustle down to first if there is a play there, so he can back up the throw.

Most of the great managers were catchers. And smart kids still prefer that position because they have the whole game in front of them, can participate in almost every play, and do as much throwing as the pitcher does, or even more.

You can't be a good catcher without a strong arm, because hard throws are an important part of your game. And of course you develop a strong arm the way a pitcher does — not by doing tricks with it but by throwing hard and throwing often. To fire the ball straight and true and fast from home plate to second base requires plenty of power in shoulder and arm, and plenty of practice to get the throws on target and get them off without delay. The thrill of nailing a fast runner at second base with a throw that zips like a gunshot right to the spot where the tag is to be made is one of the greatest thrills in the game. It is like firing a third strike, or driving a ball over the fence. And it can do your club just as much good as either of these mighty deeds. Often a bang-bang put-out like that will lift the whole club out of a low spot and set the whole gang to chattering and yelling encouragement to each other. It also can work wonders for a pitcher's morale when a pesky runner is removed from his sight.

A catcher does not throw the way a pitcher does. He doesn't have time. He must start his throw the instant he receives the pitch in his glove. He must cock his arm quickly and fire the ball fast. The reach back cannot be the generous leaning back of the body to pick the ball off that imaginary table. The catcher reaches back only

part of the length of his arm, getting his throwing hand well behind his shoulder, cocking the forearm at right angles to the upper arm, and then throwing from there. The wrist should be slightly cocked before the throw, to attain that extra speed and accuracy. But accuracy is not what the catcher learns first. *First* he learns to throw hard and fast. A catcher who has not fired many a ball into center field while he was learning is just not going to develop his arm properly.

In the beginning, as you practice throws to second base and try to get the ball to the fielder right at the base, you should let the ball fly full strength and not fret too much if it goes high over the man's head. Accuracy comes with lots of practice. If you fret over your aim and begin to try to steer the ball, you will never develop strength to get the ball to the base in a straight line and on the fly.

Of course, while these hard fast throws to second base are perhaps the most fun, your primary job as catcher is *catching* — stopping the pitches with your glove and hanging on to them. And you have to find the right stance behind the plate to do that work.

A good part of your catching will be done in a half crouch, a position that enables you to help the pitcher determine the strike zone. Your glove will be his target. (Sometimes, if your pitcher has good control, you may want to mislead the batter by holding the glove high and calling the batter's attention to its position by patting it with your bare hand, then quickly shifting it to a low position.) You make a good target by holding your glove with the whole surface facing the pitcher. Some catchers hold the rim of the glove with the bare hand, as a way of reminding themselves to keep the fingers folded. But whatever way you grip the glove be sure you present the whole surface wide open toward the pitcher. Don't show him just the edge of the glove. Give him the whole thing to aim at. And by centering your glove against your body, you provide a good bull's-eye.

In receiving the pitch you must train yourself to keep your bare hand out of the way. The catcher does his catching with one hand. Most catchers nowadays use a glove that is made for one-handed catching, a break-rim glove that can be folded over quickly to squeeze the ball.

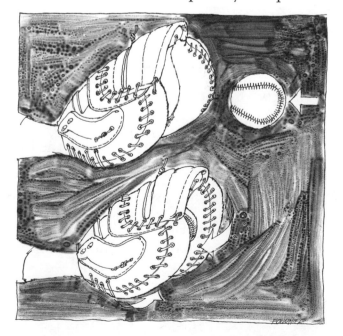

Even those catchers who still use the old-fashioned glove will keep the meat hand out of the way, fingers loosely folded (*not* clenched) until the ball hits the glove. Then they will quickly smother the ball with the bare hand to keep it from popping free.

One bad habit that may come from using the break-rim glove and taking all the pitches one-handed is catching the low pitches "from the top" — that is, holding the fingers up and pulling the ball down as you catch it. When you do that, you may take the ball right out of the strike zone and cause the umpire to call it wrong. Of course the umpire should not make such a mistake, for he is supposed to call the ball according to where it crosses the plate. But umpires are often influenced by where a ball is caught. So you must take care to influence them in the right direction, by getting those fingers down and taking the ball with an upward move.

The catcher of course signals the pitcher in advance of every pitch, or at least pretends to do so. I say "pretends" because sometimes a pitcher will call his own pitch. He does this because perhaps he has confidence in only one particular pitch, or because he knows something about the batter the catcher does not know. No matter who is calling the pitch, the catcher always goes into a full crouch to give his signals. He uses his fingers — usually one for the fast ball and two for the curve and maybe a closed fist or all four fingers for a change of pace — by laying them right against the inside of his right thigh. When you are catching, don't dangle your fingers down below your legs, or everybody on the enemy bench and many of the people in the stands will see the sign. Keep your glove at your left knee and hold it low enough so the third-base coach cannot see the sign. Give

the sign quickly and get into position to receive the pitch.

If there is ever any question about what to throw, you have to let the pitcher make the final decision. Don't ask him to throw a pitch he has no confidence in. And if there is doubt in your mind or his, go out to the mound and talk it over. Make sure he knows why you want a certain pitch. But don't get into a hassle with him. He has to have *confidence*.

You have to have confidence too, especially in throwing

to bases. You can't afford to fret about your accuracy or wonder whether you can get the throw down there in time. Any time there is a runner on base, you should be ready and eager to throw. As you take the pitch in your glove, cover it with your bare hand and let it ride, in one complete motion right up by your right ear. You then will have the ball almost in throwing position with *every* pitch. If you see the runner has taken liberties by going too far up the baseline with the pitch, step right out, making sure as you step that the baseman is ready to take a throw, and fire the ball hard to the base. Sometimes when the man has not taken too big a lead, or when there is another runner ready to go, you may just want to bluff a throw. But don't decide to throw and then change your mind halfway through. If there is a man to take the throw, let it fly. Be confident. And be aggressive. That way, you will teach the runners to respect your arm.

There have been catchers who threw snap throws without even coming out of the crouch. But leave that fancy work to the pros with the atomic arms. When you throw, step right out of the chute toward the base and let fly with a big generous stride in the direction of the throw. If your arm still lacks full strength, take three or four steps toward the target and throw *hard*.

You are likely to have to throw when the pitch is a bit wild and does not come straight into your glove. You should bear in mind that, on any wild pitch — into the dirt, for instance — the important thing is not to field the ball but to *stop* it. Always move to get your body in front of the ball. If the pitch is wide to your right, do not try a fancy stretch with the glove turned over. Hop out there, moving your *right* foot first, and get your body in front of the pitch. If you keep the ball in front of you, you have the best chance of holding the runner from advancing.

If the ball hits the dirt in front of the plate, just remember you are not an infielder and do not need to field it cleanly. Drop to your knees in front of the ball and use your glove to close up the opening between your knees, so you present a solid wall to keep the ball from getting through.

When you return the ball to the pitcher, never lob it to him, particularly when you have a runner on base. Throw it back to him straight and hard. Move out from behind the plate occasionally before you return the ball.

Talk to the pitcher and the infielders to keep the club working together. Whatever you do, don't dig in behind the plate. Your stance should be solid and comfortable, feet spread, with one foot perhaps a little in front of the other to give you good balance. Don't allow yourself to get locked into a crouch. Don't ever get your elbows between your knees. Move out and around from time to time, so you will begin to feel thoroughly at home behind the plate, ready to move out to throw, field a bunt, catch a pop foul, or back up a throw.

If your pitcher begins to get a little wild, he will probably start getting the ball too high. You can help him by giving him a really low target. Go to one knee if you have to, and set that glove right close to the ground. But remember: Don't try to catch low pitches with the fingers up. On a pitch below the waist, turn your fingers down so there will be no danger of having the ball bounce off the heel of the glove.

You can also help the pitcher by not letting him work too fast. Most good hitters, being eager to hit, like to have the pitcher work fast. So generally it is a good idea to keep the batter waiting a bit. And when a pitcher starts to lose control, or gets upset over a long hit, you should try to calm him down by holding on to the ball a little longer between pitches, even carrying the ball out to him occasionally.

If your pitcher, in his eagerness to get to the next pitch, forgets there is a man on base, it is up to you to remind him by pointing right at the man, so the pitcher will not forget to check the runner's lead.

One of the hardest jobs a young catcher has is learning not to be shy of the batter. Take your stance just as close behind the plate as the batter's swing will allow. If the batter stands up front in the batter's box, you can edge an inch or two closer to the plate. If he takes a stance deep in the box, you can back off a little, just enough so you will be clear of his swing.

It is only natural that you should blink occasionally when the bat swings in front of you, because it takes time to get used to the fact that your mask and body protector and fat glove will keep you from getting the least bit hurt. If you train yourself, as you must, to keep that bare hand out of the way, even behind your back, you will not get the kind of finger injuries catchers used to specialize in. In the ancient days, when catchers used only thin, fingerless gloves, every catcher sported two handfuls of crooked broken fingers. But nowadays, a split or broken finger means that the catcher has not been using his hands correctly. Would you believe that Elston Howard, one of the greatest New York Yankee catchers, went through his whole career without once getting a finger broken or split by a pitch or a foul tip?

Catching those foul tips is wonderful fun, once you have acquired, through practice, the confidence you need to keep your eye on that ball every second. Have faith in your mask. The ball *cannot* break through it. Keep your meat hand out of the way. And watch that ball right into your big glove. Skill at catching foul tips means lots of strikeouts for your pitcher. As you know, a third strike that tips the bat and goes directly into the catcher's glove is an out — unless the catcher drops the ball.

A good fast-ball pitcher may cause your glove hand to sting a little, especially after a few innings of steady pounding. Some catchers like to keep one finger outside the glove to ease the pounding on the first joints. (In a big glove the ball hits the fingers and not the palm of the hand.) And don't be ashamed to stick a piece of sponge rubber inside the glove to ease the impact. Big leaguers do that!

Of course you *do* get your bare hand into action when the ball strikes the glove. Then you bring it out to meet the glove and snuggle the ball as you bring both hands up over your right shoulder into throwing position.

If you do not take your stance close to the plate, as close as the batter's swing allows, you are going to be in trouble on bunts in front of the plate. You are usually the first man who knows when a bunt is coming. You can't fail to notice when the batter squares around for a sacrifice bunt. But you will also be able to observe the shift of the rear foot when the batter is going to drag a bunt or push one out in an attempt to get on base. Then you have to be ready to bound out after that ball like a cat. Don't try to "umpire" the ball. Maybe you think it's a foul ball. Get after it anyway and let the umpire decide what it is. He may disagree with you!

On all bunts except those that go up the third baseline, you should trail the ball to the *left*. That will keep you in position to get off your throw to first without turning around. Do not try to watch the batter. You *know* where he is going. Keep your eye right on the ball until you have it in your bare hand. Use your glove to round up the ball. *Never* try to pluck it up in fancy-dan manner, with a sweep of the bare hand. Use *both* hands on it. Get it securely in your bare hand. Face the bag. Be sure there is someone there to take the throw. Then throw to *him,* inside the baseline, shoulder-high.

On a sacrifice bunt there is sometimes a chance to get the runner at second, provided you get hold of the ball within two strides. But be *sure* there is a play. Better to get one out at first than to miss both outs by making a hopeless throw to second. Sometimes another player will shout to you what base to throw to. But even then, be sure there is a fielder to throw to before you let go of the ball.

On a bunt down the third baseline, you do best to trail the ball to the *right.* You will get to the ball much more quickly that way and you won't have to make a sidearm throw. Then when you have the ball securely in hand, you will be standing almost with your back to the pitcher and a half turn will bring you into position to throw overhand to first. If a bunted ball rolls right down the baseline, the best play is to let it roll. The instant it wanders into foul territory, brush it away! Don't try to make a quick pickup on a foul bunt. Nobody can advance on it anyway. Make sure it is good and foul before you pick it up. And the best way to do that is to brush it right off the diamond, once it gets into foul territory. Leave it alone and it may roll back fair again — and everybody will be safe!

If the bunted ball is too far out for you to field quickly, let the pitcher or the infielder have it. Shout loud and clear: "Take it!" so they won't wait for you to pick it up. If pitcher and infielder are both after the ball, shout out which one should field it. You can call out what base he should throw to, also. Just be sure there is going to be someone there to take the throw.

The catcher also captains the play on a throw in from the outfield to the plate. On such throws there will be a cutoff man — an infielder — standing partway up the baseline, ready to cut off the throw and go for the play at second or third, conceding the score to the lead runner. Because you will be in the best position for sizing up the chance of a play at the plate, you will have to decide if the throw should come through to you or be cut off by the infielder. Make up your mind quickly and then shout it out, good and loud: "Cut it off!" or "Let it go!"

Making the put-out at the plate is the play that gives most young catchers trouble. Some think they have to bull it out with the runner, blocking the plate with their whole bodies to keep the runner from getting near it. And some youngsters, shy of a collision, will try to make a dainty tag from a yard away.

First of all, bear in mind that you cannot, under the rules, block the baseline when you are not holding the ball. If you interfere with the base runner in such circumstances, the score counts anyway. But you can, and should, on a throw from the infield or from a relay man, stand in front of the plate, taking care to leave a slice of it open for the runner. Then, as you receive the throw, your move will depend on where the runner is. If he is well off the plate, move up the baseline to meet him, with your entire hand wrapped tight around the ball, so it cannot be jarred loose. *Never* try to hold the ball in the glove alone. Get your whole bare hand around it, *tight*. If the runner comes straight at you, slow him down with your glove hand, then lay the ball on him and hop out of his way. Don't get into a wrestling match with him or try to show him how tough you are.

If the runner is close, you will have to drop down to one knee so he cannot slide under the tag. You can put one foot in front of the plate, where it will prevent a sliding foot from hooking the plate, and put the ball down where his slide will bring him right into it. But when you take that position, be sure you have a tight hold of the ball. If you don't have the ball, you have got to leave the plate open to the runner.

If it is a long throw that may come into the plate on the bounce, the place to wait for it is behind the plate. You can jump forward to meet the runner when you have secured the ball in your bare hand. Perhaps the toughest put-out to make at the plate is on a throw from right field. You have *got* to keep your eye on the ball

first of all or it may get away from you. Yet you must be aware of the runner too, or he may slide in and take your feet right out from under you. On this play, you have got to use the kind of split vision a basketball player uses, as he makes ready to pass to a moving teammate without tipping off the direction of the pass. You will be looking at the ball, but you should have the runner in the corner of your eye and be ready to clear out if he gets there before the throw does. Of course if you get the throw in time for the put-out you may have to drop right to your knees to meet him.

Whatever you do, don't let a runner intimidate you. There are really very few times that you will actually collide with a runner if you play your position correctly. Sometimes when the throw comes in late you may not have time to take a good tight grip on the ball. Then you should be especially careful to make the tag with *both* hands, protecting the ball with the glove. If you have your left foot properly placed, in front of the corner of the plate the runner must tag, you can brace yourself by setting your right foot a little behind the other. Then no matter how the runner slides, you can tag him before he scores. If he comes straight in, you have a shin guard to keep you from getting injured by his spikes. If he falls away and tries to hook the plate, your foot will prevent his foot from getting to the plate. And you can get the ball down there quickly, in both hands, to tag him.

If you meet the runner up the baseline, as you should when the throw gets to you ahead of his slide, you have a right to keep the runner off you by putting out your glove hand to slow him down. Then you just tag him with the ball clenched tight, and jump out of there.

Of course if the throw is well off target, you cannot just stand by the plate and watch it go. You must go meet it, wherever it is. You'll have to concede the score — although sometimes, if the runner does not get a good jump, you may be able, with a quick dive, to put the tag on. But even if the man scores, you have to look for a play at some other base. Don't waste time griping to yourself about a bad throw or a lost score. Look for the *next* play. That may be the one that means the ball game.

When you have men on base, it is up to you to keep them from getting too big a lead and to nail them when you can. So you must not only remind your pitcher when he has a base runner to deal with, you must keep the runners in mind yourself. Sometimes, when you suspect the other side is going to put a play on, you can find out by signaling for a pitch-out — a pitch so far out of the strike zone the batter could not reach it if he wanted to. Say there is a runner on third, with less than two out; the game is close, with one run needed to tie or go ahead; and there is a weak hitter (or an expert bunter) at bat. There is a good chance the other side may call a squeeze play here. You can find out by asking immediately for a pitch-out. If there *is* a play on and the runner starts from third on the pitch, you'll have him trapped. If he has come far down the line however, get him started back before you throw the ball to third.

When you feel sure a steal or a hit-and-run is on, a pitch-out can enable you to nail the runner. Or it can show you if the batter is planning to bunt.

Bluff throws, too, can often help you break up the other guy's strategy. They work best on a double steal, when there are runners on first and third. The runner on first, when this play is on, will break for second base on the pitch. The runner on third base then has got to start for home as *soon* as the catcher lets the ball go to second. He can't wait to make sure. He has to start the instant the catcher throws. So if you can make a really convincing bluff throw to second, you may trap the runner yards off the base. But it can't be a half-hearted bluff. It has to look real. Take a tight grip on the ball with your whole hand, charge out of the chute and fire with all your might *exactly* as you do on a steal — except that you *hold on to the ball!* Then look at the runner on third. Make sure there is a fielder covering the bag (sometimes the third baseman may charge in, anticipating a bunt). Then snap a fast throw down there.

The best time to pick a runner off base is right after a swinging strike. Most runners will make several swift steps toward the next base when the batter swings, and if you are alert, you can catch them too far off and leaning in the wrong direction. That is why you must get that ball up into throwing position every time you receive a pitch. Make that a normal part of your motion, to carry that ball right up behind your ear.

The art of catching fouls is one that young catchers often pay too little attention to. Yet catching a foul may save a ball game by getting a dangerous runner out of there. Too many times, a missed foul fly that gives the batter another chance to swing leads to a big hit. So you must scramble after every pop foul you have any chance for. As soon as that ball flies off the bat into the air, start after it. Get your mask off with one quick upward sweep of your right hand. And *hold on* to the mask until you have located the ball. Then toss the mask away from the spot where the ball is going to drop. If the ball has gone straight up, get yourself under the ball — right under it, so it seems to be coming down on your nose. The natural spin on the ball will carry it a little away from you. It is a good idea to catch foul balls with the glove high — about face-level. Foul pops have a lot of spin and they can hop right out of a glove in a split second. If your glove is high, you will have another chance to grab the ball before it hits the ground.

Foul pops usually veer pretty far off a straight line as they drop, especially if they are close to high stands, where there are air currents that will push them away from the stands. When you chase a ball to the stands, let it lead you a little. You can make a quick adjustment with your glove if the ball curves away, and it is easier to reach forward than to back up. But if you have merely tried to hold your glove under it, it may come down well beyond your reach.

Remember, too, that if there is a runner on base, he can advance at his own risk after the catch, just as he can after a fair fly ball caught in the outfield. Sometimes, when there is a great distance between you and the backstop and a foul fly is going to require you to make a catch at top speed, with your back to the plate and far out of position, it may be better to let the ball drop than to give the runner a good chance to score. In most ball parks, of course, you seldom have to chase a foul ball so far behind the plate that you get out of easy range. But stay alive always to the chance that a man may be running after the catch.

One aspect of the catcher's job that adds a lot to the fun and satisfaction is the chance to use your brains — to outthink the enemy as well as to outplay him. The catcher does not do all the pitcher's thinking for him, because the pitcher himself must take each batter as a separate job of work and plan ways of getting him out, or getting him to hit into an out or a double play. The catcher is in a position to observe many things that a pitcher might miss, and the catcher also can tell better than the pitcher himself when the pitcher is tiring or losing control of one of his pitches.

Basically, the strategy of a pitcher-catcher combination is to make the batter go for the get-him-out pitch, to hit the pitcher's pitch. The batter of course is out there looking for *his* pitch. So what you and the pitcher try to do, ordinarily, is to get the batter into a spot where he has *got* to swing at what you want him to go for. To do that, of course, you have to know a good deal about the batter's strengths and weaknesses, as well as his preferences. In amateur ball it is not always possible to know all that about a batter, so you have to keep your eyes open for signs that will give away what the batter is planning or what sort of pitch he likes.

As I have already mentioned, a batter's stance often gives an idea of what kind of pitch he prefers. A study of the batters in batting practice will enable you to pick out the bad ball hitters, the players who will hit a ball where it is pitched, and the hitters who are out to break the ball in two. It is a pretty sure bet that the hefty swingers like fast balls and like them high. You can start them off with a curve. The batters who choke up a little and use an abbreviated swing can often handle curve balls the best. In amateur ball, it must be noted, there are not too many batters who can hit a curve successfully, but you are bound to find a few. Anyway, part of your job is to get to know the enemy batters, to pick out the players who swing late (there are a lot of those around in amateur and school baseball), the players who pull the ball and the ones who are addicted to topping the ball and getting it on the ground.

In the actual game, you will soon discover which guys are overeager to hit and will go for the first ball every time, as well as the hitters who are a little gun-shy and can be scared away from the plate with a cross-fire pitch — a sidearm pitch that comes from the extreme pitching-hand corner of the plate. (A right-handed pitcher cannot, of course, use a cross fire on a left-handed batter, nor can a left-hander scare a right-handed batter that way.) You can watch and see which guys will dig in at the plate and which guys will shift their stances continually. As a general rule, the diggers-in are the confident hitters, while the hitters who keep the rear foot shifting around are the slap-and-poke hitters, who don't care much for inside pitches.

All this information will help you as you plan your strategy and will make the whole game twice as interesting and exciting. But of course you have to tell your pitcher about your thinking, so he will have confidence in his pitches. So talk to your pitcher frequently, tell him what you have figured out about certain batters and remind him about how he handled a batter the previous time. You must also take care that neither of you gets into a rut with your calls. The standard routine may be high-inside, low-outside; or fast ball, curve, fast ball, curve. Be sure you break that routine every now and then. Remember, no matter what his coach may tell him, the batter is going to be guessing with the pitcher, and if you always follow the same pattern, he will have it figured out quickly.

When you observe from his shift in stance that a batter is planning to bunt, or when you know a bunt is in order, do not make the mistake of trying to keep the ball away from the batter, so he can't bunt it. You don't want to walk him just to keep him from sacrificing. Just don't make his job too easy. Let him bunt. But let him bunt *your* pitch. Low pitches are hard to bunt. A lot of amateur batters can't seem to bend their knees enough to get the bat in the way of a low pitch. Tight pitches

are hard to bunt, too. The tight, inside pitch, as I
mentioned before, is the one to use when a squeeze play
is likely, and there is a right-handed batter up. If the
batter is left-handed, and you want to break up a suicide
squeeze, when the batter *must* hit the ball, you give him
a pitch well outside, so he will have to cross the plate
to get his bat on it. When he crosses the plate he is
automatically out and the runner cannot score.

I pointed out earlier that big, hungry hitters, when
they are obviously straining to break up the game with
one big swing, will often swing at a ball that is right in
the dirt in front of the plate. A catcher must not be
chicken about calling for such a pitch when it is needed.
(You can signal for such a pitch by simply pointing into
the dirt after you have given your regular sign. Likewise,
you can call for inside or outside, by placing your bare
hand on the knee on the side desired, and for a high
pitch by pointing upward.) One thing you must keep
in mind about an into-the-dirt pitch is that, when the
batter has two strikes on him and he swings and misses
on such a pitch, he can run to first at his own risk. A
pitch that bounces in front of the plate is not "fairly
caught" under the rules, even if it bounces right into

your glove. So be ready to throw on such a pitch as soon as you get it into your hand.

Besides studying the batter, the catcher has to study his own pitcher. As you warm up with your pitcher, you should take special note of just how his good pitch is acting. If he has a curve he likes to throw and he is not getting it into the strike zone, you should get him to agree that you will use this only for a "waste" pitch, until he can begin to put it into the strike zone. (Often in a game, a pitcher's control will begin to improve after an inning or two.) A waste pitch is one thrown out of the strike zone, chiefly to keep the batter off balance and remind him he cannot count on getting the same pitch every time.

Every pitcher has one pitch that is especially effective. In your warm-up you have to make sure he can control this pitch and that it is acting the way you want it to — breaking properly or sizzling into your glove with the proper zip. If his best pitch is right, that is the pitch you and the pitcher want to count on in tight spots. With men on base, the tying or winning run in scoring position, a full count on a strong batter, the potential third out in the last inning, you should try never to allow your pitcher to try something cute — no trick pitches, off-speed pitches, or hard-to-control pitches. Go with your best! And tell him to throw hard.

The catcher also has to keep watch to see when a pitcher is tiring or getting careless. A pitcher often first shows his fatigue when he begins to pitch without bending his back — "pitching straight up" is what the pros call it — or when he is failing to get his arm well up over his head as he makes the pitch. Sometimes this is not real fatigue but just a failure on the pitcher's part to concentrate all his strength on the job. Concentration in baseball does not mean merely focusing your mind on the job, but your full strength as well. Every athlete has reserve strength that he can use only through an act of will. It is like the effort you can exert when you fail on your first try to complete some simple feat — jumping over an obstacle, breaking a stick, lifting a heavy package. You gather yourself together and decide you are going to give it a *good* try. And suddenly you find the strength to do it. A careless pitcher or a tired pitcher may have to be reminded to dig into that reserve, to tell himself: *Throw hard!* Throw HARD!

Tell him what he is doing wrong: He is not coming

over the top with his fast ball. He is not bending his back into the pitch. He is unconsciously shortening his stride. And remind him that he *can* do better and has been doing better earlier.

Obviously, a catcher has to be something of a psychologist or have some understanding of human nature to get the best work out of a pitcher. In amateur ball, you will probably be working with the same pitcher almost all the time, so you should be able to learn pretty quickly how to prompt him to do his best. Some pitchers have to be needled a little. Some have to be flattered. There are some young pitchers who will lose their cool very quickly if they give up a hit and then get criticized for it. You have to be gentle with those types and feed them plenty of simple flattery. Tell them the batter was lucky. Blame yourself for a bad call. Tell them their best pitch is unhittable and that the next batter is probably going to pop to the infield. Remind them there is a whole club behind them who will keep those runners from advancing.

Then there are other types who can't seem to keep their minds on the job, who like to fool around and take careless chances. You may really have to jab the needle into them, to tell them that the whole club is counting on them, that the fans are making fun of them, that *you* don't think they are throwing nearly as hard as they could.

Every pitcher is a special case and needs individual treatment. But *every* pitcher likes to be told how good he is, even if he pretends not to like it. When your pitcher is working well, be sure to keep telling him so. When he comes through with a good pitch to make a crucial out, give him plenty of applause.

And you have to keep the rest of the club playing hard too. Don't allow any player to get down on himself because he makes an error, or even two or three. Make it your job to buck him up, to tell him to forget it, to get the next batter, to hang in there and show the crowd how he can *really* play.

One of the hardest pitchers to deal with is the one who just does not want *anyone* to tell him what to do. Not many players like this get into organized baseball, or stay there very long, unless they have extraordinary talent. But often in amateur ball you will find a pitcher who will keep shaking off signs, for no real reason except that he wants to do things his own way. You have to talk to fellows like this and make them feel that they *are* doing it their way. If you see a batter edging a bit closer to the plate, obviously looking for the curve, you may have to go out and ask the pitcher if he hasn't noticed that and if he doesn't think it might be fun to fool the batter with a fast ball.

If a pitcher is stubborn, however, don't get into an argument with him. He has to be convinced that what he is doing is right or he may not put his heart into it.

When you are working with a curve-ball pitcher you may notice that, as he gets tired, his curve will begin to "hang" — to go through the strike zone about chest-high, instead of breaking down and away as it should. It may be that he is not giving himself enough "air" to work in — not reaching up high enough on his delivery to provide the room he needs to put spin on the ball. If you can't cure a guy of that trouble by telling him about it and urging him to give it a *real* try, you can often help him (if there are no runners on base) by giving him an extra-low target, that is, by going to one knee and putting the rim of the glove right on the ground.

I don't believe young pitchers should throw knuckle-balls. They are not hard to throw but they are devilish to catch and you should talk your pitcher out of trying them. Throwing stuff like this will interfere with the development of a pitcher's arm, by getting him in the habit of pushing the ball instead of throwing it and of putting only part of the length of his arm into play. So you not only have to throw hard yourself to get the good out of the game, you have to keep reminding your pitcher to do the same. Of course, he will use off-speed pitches from time to time to keep the batter off balance. But essentially his job is to throw hard. And your job is to remind him to do so.

Often if you are working with a really good pitcher, you will find that he has some new pitch he wants to try out. Talk him out of using it in dangerous situations or against a batter who is especially strong. And promise to call it every now and then when you are well ahead of the batter, have a good lead in the game, or have no runners on base. The only way he is going to make a new pitch work is by using it in a game and you have to give him that chance. Tell him how it's working. Don't tell him it's *bad*, but if it is missing the strike zone, suggest it needs more work and you will use it as a waste pitch for a while.

You will find that many pitchers tend to ease up when

they are working against the lower part of the batting order, the guys who are not supposed to be able to hit the ball safely more than once in five or six trips. Or they will begin to get fancy when they have a good lead and think the time has come to show off some trick pitches. You have to urge those guys to *throw strikes* at such times. Having a good lead means that you can afford to challenge every hitter, to force him to hit to get on base. And the bottom of the batting order is the place where the K's (strikeouts) grow. Sometimes a weak hitter won't be able to hit anything *but* a trick, off-speed pitch. Or he may be so reluctant to swing that he will get himself a walk just by watching all the fancy pitches go by. Tell your pitcher to have no mercy on those hitters. Wipe them out!

Catchers have to deal with umpires more than any other player. One thing you should tell yourself is that you are not going to do yourself or your club any good by getting a reputation as a guy who is always *on* the umpires. Umpires will often unconsciously give such a player the worst of it. And you can get your pitcher all upset if you instigate some big argument over an umpire's call. As a matter of fact, part of the catcher's job should be to keep the pitcher from getting into a temper fit over an umpire's call. The pitcher more than anyone else on the club can be infuriated by an umpire's mistake, because it may destroy a carefully planned bit of strategy that had worked (the pitcher thought) to perfection — a strikeout perhaps with two out and the tying run on third base. But a pitcher can sometimes become so infuriated with the umpire that he will lose his control completely and will start missing the strike zone by a foot or more on every pitch.

Most pitchers just need a little time to cool off after a blow-off with an umpire, and you should hasten to get out there and help give him that time. Remind him that he can't let one pitch ruin the whole game, that the whole club is ready to help him make up for that, that it won't even things up at all to let the game get away from him now, that the umpire will probably give *him* a break next time. Even if you don't agree that it was a bad call, tell him you think it was, that the umpire blew it, but that it will take more than a few bad calls to spoil the great job he is doing. And so on. Pat his back. Praise him. And stay with him until he stops sputtering. Then be sure he works slowly and throws hard.

There are certain standard tactics the catcher should know the value of. With a two-strike, no-ball count on the batter, for instance, it is almost always best to throw the next pitch out of the strike zone, assuming that the batter is going to be ready to swing at anything near the plate. Weak hitters will often forget the need to "guard the plate" and once in a great while you can blow a fast ball past them in that situation. But experienced batters are going to be swinging at anything that might be called a strike, and you want to take advantage of that attitude.

In a tight ball game, or a game in which your club is behind, you have to treat the dangerous hitters with respect. If a slugger comes up with a man on second, or men on second and third, you will not be a great deal worse off if he is on first base. You will at least then have a force-out at every base and a potential double play. You may not want to walk such a man, especially if his run would put the other side ahead, but you can "pitch around" him. That is, you can ask your pitcher to throw stuff in, out, high, low — just out of the strike zone or where the batter cannot get good solid wood on the ball. He'll be eager to hit and may very well take a cut at a bad pitch that will give you an easy out. At worst, he will get a walk and you'll have another chance to get the side out without damage.

But this does not mean that you should let any batter scare you. Perhaps your pitcher may show signs of nervousness when a batter comes up who got a solid hit off him last time, or who has a reputation as the top hitter on the club. Ask your pitcher to give this sort of batter his *best* pitch at the outer edge of the strike zone. If he is a pull hitter, as most of the long-ball boys are, this will be a pitch he is least likely to hurt you on. At the same time you don't want to let his reputation scare you out of the strike zone altogether.

The catcher can do a great deal to help his club if he is aware of what the batter will probably try to do. Of course, as I said, you can often discover a batter's intentions with a pitch-out. But there are situations when you should know, without investigation, what the batter is likely to try to accomplish. If, for instance, there is nobody out, with a runner on second base, you can be pretty sure the batter is going to try to move the runner to third with a hit to right field. So your pitcher should be trying to get the batter to hit ahead of the runner, so the runner will have to hold his ground for a while before trying to advance. He can do that best by feeding a right-handed hitter tight pitches, and offering outside pitches to a left-hander. And of course, when you are using this strategy, you must be sure the rest of the club is backing it up. If you are trying to make the man hit to left, you don't want your left fielder to be pulled far over to center to leave wide open spaces for the ball to drop in.

When the winning run is on third base with less than two out in the last of the ninth, you have got to watch out for *short* fly balls or line drives to the outfield. A *long* fly ball is going to score that run whether it is caught or not, so what you have to fear is the fly ball just over the infield, or the line drive that may fall in front of the outfielder. Make sure, in these circumstances, that the outfielders are drawn well in to cover the short area, where a caught fly cannot score a run.

In a tight ball game, with a man on third and less than two out, your infielders will generally be playing in over the baselines to make it easier to cut off that run. When your infielders are shortened up this way, they leave a wide area where a batter can dump a looping drive safely. So you have to make sure your pitcher keeps the ball *low*, to increase the possibility of a ground ball. High pitches are the ones batters can most easily dump into the open areas behind the drawn-in fielders.

Of course no one can lay down a list of rules that will cover every possible situation that may face a catcher in a baseball game. The game is just too full of surprises for that. But if you stay alert at all times and maintain an *aggressive* attitude, you will be ready for anything that may happen and you will greatly increase the fun you get out of the game.

As a matter of fact, you can set the whole tone of the game if you show aggressiveness at every stage. There used to be a big-league catcher who would start every game by running out to his position and punching his fist high, yelling, "Let's go!" It used to lift everyone's spirits just to see how much joy he was getting out of baseball. You can accomplish the same end by talking things up to your infield, moving out of your position from time to time, keeping an eye on the base runners at all times, and being ready, when any runner takes liberties, to fire the ball down to *any* base. A loose-limbed and mobile catcher who does not let himself get locked into his position is not only great fun to watch. He himself, by playing with his whole heart every minute and by throwing that ball *hard* and fast when he sees a chance for an out, gets twice as much fun out of playing.

The First Baseman

It used to be, many years ago, that the first baseman was just a guy who stood with one foot on first base and took all the throws. He was not expected to do any real throwing at all. Indeed, one old-time first baseman, Jake Beckley of Pittsburgh, who was named the best of his day, had the weakest throwing arm in all baseball, so weak that he could not throw a man out from first base to home, or even from partway down the baseline. Once, when Jake had the ball in his hand, a runner on third who knew about his arm broke for home. Jake, realizing he would never throw the man out, started full speed for home himself. Luckily, he was a really fast man afoot and he got within range just as the runner started to slide. So Jake simply hurled himself through the air and landed on the runner, bringing him to a dead stop short of home plate. He broke three of the runner's ribs. And he made the put-out.

But ever since the days of Charles Comiskey in St. Louis, in the 1880s, or of Fred Tenney in Boston a few years later, the first baseman has gradually become a thrower, for these men helped perfect the combination infield plays that made the first baseman something more than a target to throw at. Of course you should not play first base if you don't enjoy catching all kinds of throws. But you should also be able to throw quickly and throw hard and throw accurately. That is, you should be able to cock your throwing arm quickly behind your shoulder and get rid of the ball fast, so that it travels in a trolley-line to its target. The infield is no place for humpbacked throws. You occasionally have to use an underhand toss to the pitcher to make a put-out. But in getting the ball from one base to another, you throw hard and fast. Slow throws give a base runner too much of an advantage.

The first baseman therefore should develop his arm just as the other players do, by throwing often and throwing hard — at targets. And, like the others, he should not be timid about making errors on throws. They say a cook learns his job by spoiling lots of food.

An infielder (like the catcher) learns his job by spoiling lots of throws. Remind yourself in all your practice not to try to steer the ball by timid use of your arm. Let her fly! Of course you have your eye on the target and your foot pointed toward the target, and you step toward the target as you throw. But you throw hard, *harder*, HARDER! Just be sure you warm your arm up, even in hot weather, and that you quit throwing the instant you feel any twinge.

In all your practice, if you intend to play first base, or have been awarded that job, you should work around a base. If you can't get a real base to practice with, draw a base in the dirt, or use a board or a flat rock. It is important that you make a habit of finding the base the instant you field a ball. You should always have a good idea of just where you are playing in relation to the base and how far you must move to get your foot on it. And remember, you get your toe on it, not your heel. If you stretch for a throw with only your heel in contact with the base, there is a good chance that you will lift your heel off the base as you take the throw and the runner will be safe.

Of course you don't put your foot in the middle of the

base where the runner will step on it. You should leave most of the base for him. But as you start your stretch, your toe should be on the base.

The first baseman nowadays, like the catcher, is a one-handed receiver. His glove does not protect his hand. It is simply a sort of basket in which the ball is to be snagged, with the fingers completely out of the pocket. Actually most players find it is more fun to catch this way. It is like catching bolts in a bucket or flying objects in a net. It takes a good deal of practice to develop the knack. But the practice is pure fun and actually the knack is not at all difficult to acquire. Once you have it, it's yours for good. Just keep your eye on the ball until you have snagged it safely.

The first baseman has to expect every throw to be a bad one, and he has to expect a throw on every ground ball that he does not try to field himself. So your first move when a ball is hit — unless *you* are going after the ball yourself — is to scramble to get to the bag. Don't make the fielder wait for you. Be at the bag, waiting for the throw, while he is fielding the ball. And because you know that the throw may be off target, do not commit yourself to any catching position before the fielder throws. Instead, stand on the second base side of the bag and look down at once to make sure just where the bag is. Stand relaxed, with your knees flexed and back bent, looking right at the ball. Hold your glove up in front of you to show the fielder a target.

Then, when the ball is on its way — and only then — you get in position to catch it. If it is coming right for you, you get your toe on the bag and *stretch* toward the throw, stepping as far out with your glove-side foot as you possibly can and reaching out the full length of your arm. The purpose of this stretch is to cut down the

distance the ball has to travel. The fraction of a second you save by getting hold of the ball a few feet off the bag may make the difference between "safe" and "out."

Don't ever get into the habit of reaching out for the throw with your elbow bent, using only part of the length of your arm. Get that big glove out just as *far* as you can put it without losing contact with the base. There was a big-league first baseman who became indignant once when his manager said he had let him go because he was a "short-armed" fielder. The player set out to prove that his arms were as long as any other man's on the club. But that is not what the manager meant. He meant that the first baseman caught throws with his glove hand slightly retracted so that he gave up about a foot of distance, with the result that some fast runners were reaching first safely when they should have been out.

Remember that the farther you reach with your glove, the faster the runner has to travel to beat the throw.

But as I said, you have to expect bad throws. In fact you should tell yourself that every throw is going to be off target. Don't start to stretch for it until you *know* it is coming within proper range of your glove. It is largely up to you to turn bad throws into good throws, so you should be ready to shift your position quickly. If the throw is too high, you may be able to bring it down by hopping quickly to the foul side of first base and shifting your feet, so the bare-hand-side toe is on the base. By getting a few feet the other side of the bag this way, you may give the throw time to drop a little so you can reach it without leaving the base. But when it comes to a clear choice between leaving the base and catching the ball, of course you leave the base. If the ball goes by, it will cost another base, or a run if there are other runners aboard. So always go get the ball.

Many throws, especially if they are hurried, will hit the dirt before they reach you. These have to be fielded as you field a ground ball (a matter we will take up in detail when we talk about the problems of infielders). That is, you must field the throw out in front of your forward foot, with your head right over the ball and your eye on the ball every second. On this play you have got to get both hands involved, to make sure you can round up the ball quickly. The easiest such throw to field is the one you can take on the short hop. These you can smother quickly and take a solid grip on at once. The harder throws are the ones that bounce well out in front of you. They do not always bounce true and may require some sudden adjustments. But if you keep your eye on the ball every moment, your hands will adjust automatically.

If you can field bad throws quickly and neatly, your teammates will be proud of you, because you'll be making them look good. And there is a lot of extra satisfaction in gobbling up throws that look as if they are going to miss. So a good part of your practice, if you are going to play first base (and that is the *only* infield position a left-hander can play), should be the fielding of bad throws. Get someone to throw you all sorts of bad throws on purpose, and especially those that hit the dirt and skip toward you. Of course you'll miss a lot of these throws. You may even miss *all* of them for a few days. But keep at them. You will get so you enjoy the thrill of gloving a bad throw and may even start to look forward to the chance to save a play in that manner.

Another really tough play to get used to is the throw that comes in on the home-plate side of first base and seems likely to hit the runner. Many fielders automatically try to get out of the runner's way on this throw, and get themselves into foul territory to make the catch.

Don't do that! Reach right down the baseline for the throw, even if the runner seems to be headed straight at you. The rules require him to run *outside* the baseline. If he runs on the line and prevents you from catching the ball, he is out anyway. So pick the ball right off his uniform if you have to. If the throw is so far down the line that you have to leave the base to get it, you may still be able to put a tag on the runner as he goes by.

If the throw is so bad it pulls you off the bag, or if you make a grab for it and it gets by, do not waste time expressing your frustration. A first baseman for the Yankees helped lose a World Series game one day when he missed a throw, by taking the time to pound the bag in anger. Meanwhile the ball was bouncing way into the outfield and the runners were taking extra bases. There are a lot of frustrations at first, not just missed throws and wild throws, but close calls by the umpire that you think should have gone your way. You can't afford to waste energy on slamming your glove around or kicking dirt. There's *another* play coming right away, and you may save the day with that.

When there are other runners on base besides the one who is trying for first, don't pause to congratulate yourself on a put-out. Look for the next play! Come right off the base ready to throw.

While the first baseman generally does not need to have the range and the fielding skill of the other in-fielders, he has plenty of chances to grab ground balls. In the big leagues, men have held their jobs at first on the power of their bats, and their fielding has been left mostly to a second baseman who could cover ground enough for two. But in amateur ball, every infielder has to do his part on defense as well as at bat.

As a first baseman your "territory" is all the ground between first and second that you can reach when a ground ball comes that way. You can help most on slow-hit ground balls, or on drag bunts that a left-handed batter uses to get on base. A drag bunt often goes straight at the second baseman, who, unless he is expecting the play, is so far behind the baseline he cannot get hold of the ball soon enough to make the put-out. But an alert and agile first baseman can sometimes get to the ball in time. You should not hesitate to poach on the second baseman's turf if he knows you can field the bunt. The second baseman then will probably cover first, or maybe the pitcher will get over there in time.

The first baseman will often field ground balls that go to his left, near the foul line, and that may draw him far from the bag. The pitcher will almost always be the man who covers the base on these plays, and you will be making the short throw to the bag. There are two important things to remember in making this throw — or toss, which is what it usually is. Number one is to get the ball to the pitcher *before* he reaches the bag. He will be running hard for the base and watching for the ball. Don't make him look for base and ball at the same time. Toss the ball so he can take it about shoulder-high while he is still two or three steps from the base. And move *toward* the base as you make the toss.

The other point to remember is that you must let the pitcher *see* the ball from the instant you start your toss. Do not try to flick the ball to him with your glove, or from behind your glove. Pull your gloved hand well out of the way so the ball does not come popping out of nowhere to the pitcher. One reason that a toss is better than a soft throw is that the ball on a toss is visible all the time, both in your hand and on its way to the pitcher.

But the first choice always is to make the put-out yourself if you possibly can. Anytime you can complete a play in baseball without a throw you are cutting down on chances for error. So if you field the ball close enough to the bag so that you *know* you can beat the runner, wave the pitcher off and go for the put-out yourself.

The first baseman is an important man on bunts, particularly sacrifice bunts, where he may have a chance of getting the lead runner. A left-handed first baseman has a distinct advantage on this play, for if he is able to field a bunt quickly — say in one or two strides, he can fire the ball to second base without turning all the way around. A right-handed first baseman *can* throw to second without turning, but it is an awkward move. He has to twist his body sharply to get his right arm well behind his shoulder for the throw. And so it is best, if he fields the ball instantly, to make a complete turn of the body before the throw. The extra speed of the throw will partly compensate for the extra time this move takes.

It really is not often, however, that a first baseman gets hold of a sacrifice bunt in time to make an out at second base. It will happen only when the bunter has tapped the ball too strongly, or when the first baseman gets a lightning jump on the ball and grabs it on the first hop. Getting a jump on the ball is not a simple matter, for with a runner on first base — and of course there usually will be one on a sacrifice bunt — the base-man will be holding the runner on and cannot (or should not) leave the base until he *knows* the pitch is going to the plate.

In any event, you should never throw blindly to second base. On any infield play, a mix-up may develop that will leave second base uncovered. So look to see that there is a fielder to take your throw. And check the runner to be sure he has not already made it to the base. Sometimes, anticipating a bunt, a runner will start on the pitcher's motion and there'll be no chance of beating him to the bag with a throw. You have to check both these matters in a split second. Then, if you know you have a play, throw overhand, hard and straight, so it will get to the fielder about shoulder-high. This is a force play, so there is no need to get the ball down for the fielder to put a tag on the runner. And once in a few hundred times, there may be a double play possible here, for some runners do not go all out for first base on a sacrifice. And if the fielder gets the ball at throwing height, he can get off a throw without delay.

Bear in mind, however, that the chance of getting the

runner at second base on a sacrifice bunt is never a good one. If there is any doubt in your mind about beating the runner with your throw, then go for the put-out at first. The pitcher will be covering there and you can turn and get off a quick throw to him, *inside* the baseline. Or if you field the ball close enough to the line you may be able to make a tag play on the runner.

You will have to spend a good part of your time at first base holding the runner on, to keep him from getting too good a start for second. When you hold the runner on, you do *not* stand between him and the base. You cannot block the baseline when you do not have the ball. Take up your stance on the outside corner of the bag, toward home, on the foul side. Stand relaxed, knees flexed, glove giving the pitcher a target. Because the pitcher will be doing his best to keep the runner from reading his intentions, you will seldom know for sure that the pitcher is going to throw to you. You have to be ready all the time, right up to the point where you can see clearly that the pitch is going to the plate. Stand ready, glove in position, and keep *wanting* that ball to come to you. When you get the throw, put the ball down immediately at the inside edge of the base, where the runner has to be coming in. But never swing your hand back without looking, and *never*, as some right-handers have done, try to swing the ball behind your back to make the tag. You may discover, to your great embarrassment, that the runner has taken off for second base and you have nobody to tag. Incidentally, if a bunt is expected, you should always signal the pitcher if you are going to charge the plate. Agree on a signal beforehand.

With a left-handed batter up, the first baseman is on the hot corner, where line drives come whistling and ground balls occasionally sizzle toward him like rockets. So the coach or manager will sometimes have him playing well behind the base, a few strides toward second, regardless of whether there is a runner on base or not. But from this position, the first baseman can sometimes work a pickoff play. And he should always be ready to hustle back to the bag after a pitch to give the catcher a chance to nail a careless runner. Runners sometimes begin to take for granted that the baseman is far away and may be inclined to "lean" a little more toward second with the pitch, and be slow about shortening their lead. An alert catcher will be looking for every chance to throw and you should help him by being ready, after every pitch goes through, to receive a throw.

The first baseman, like all other infielders, needs plenty of practice at fielding ground balls. The best practice is to get lots of ground balls right off the bat, under game conditions. But short of that, you should get out as often as you can, and put in as much time as you can, for infield practice when the coach or a teammate hits balls with the fungo bat. Don't settle for a few soft taps in your direction. Ask the batter to bang them down your way as sharply as he can, so you can learn to handle all sorts of bounces. To field a ground ball properly, you must move right in on it whenever you can. Of course, there will be balls that come at you so fast that you will have no chance but to give ground a step to get the hop you want. Generally, however, you must make your own hop by charging right toward the ball to field it in front of your forward foot, in your natural stride, with *both* hands.

If you watch a lot of amateur baseball you will discover that most ground balls that get away from infielders go under their gloves. For some reason young players are hesitant about getting down low enough to field a ground ball properly. They will either try to get

down with back straight, or they will bend over with
stiff knees to reach down to the ball. To field a ground
ball properly, however, you must *bend your knees* and
bend your back. Dig your glove right into the dirt for
the ball. The best point to field a ground ball is the short
hop. You should move in on the ball and try to smother
it just as it leaves the ground. Keep your head right down
over the ball — not turned away or lifted to see where
you are going to throw. Big-league managers tell young
players to get their heads down so they can see the bills
of their caps when they are fielding a ground ball. It
just stands to reason that you cannot adjust your hands
to the bounce of a fast-moving ball unless you have your
eye right on it. But if you do have your eye on the ball,
your hands will adjust automatically to a bad bounce or
a sudden skittering along the ground. Just remember
that you are playing the ball and go after it with the idea
of smothering it on the short hop. Don't let it play you by
forcing you to back off in hopes of getting a high bounce.

One move you should always avoid is any effort to
"round up" a ground ball in order to reach it when it
is bouncing well. Cut straight across the path of the ball
and try to get your hands on it as fast as you can, as if all

the rest of the world was trying to beat you to it. Get your body as low as you can, and dig right into the dirt after the ball. In the days when big leaguers played on real gravel, they often brought up a ground ball with gravel trickling out of the glove. Once you have the ball securely in your hand, come up throwing! That is, as you get out of your crouch, bring your throwing hand right up behind your shoulder, ready to let fly.

The first baseman seldom has a really long throw to make, except when it is necessary to cut off a run at the plate or relay an outfield throw to third. Those throws should always be made overhand. You may be able to get off a sidearm throw more quickly. But it lacks the speed of an overhand throw and it usually veers so far off a straight line that the receiver may have trouble with it, especially against a difficult background. You can afford to give up the tiny saving on time in return for more zip and accuracy.

In amateur ball, a double play made from first to second and back to first is about as common as a left-handed catcher. But it is often necessary, when you have a slow runner on the baselines, for the first baseman, after he fields a ground ball, to go to second with his throw. A left-hander has little trouble with this throw, for he is in throwing position as he fields the ball. But a right-hander often has to twist his body awkwardly to get the throw off to second. It can be done, however, by pivoting quickly, with the left knee dipping almost to the ground, to get the arm back far enough to give some power to the throw. But the best way for a right-hander, when he fields the ball close to the foul line, is to follow the swing of his body all the way around to the left so he faces second base and can throw naturally.

Most of the time, with a run in scoring position and a ball hit to deep right field, the first baseman must act as cutoff man. The cutoff man is not to be confused with the relay man, who runs out on the grass to take a throw from the outfielder. The cutoff man *must* play inside the diamond. He has to know where the base runners are, which means he has to be able to keep them in view without turning around. His job is to cut off the out-fielder's throw when he is told to, and try to nail a runner at either second or third. This is an extremely important job. There have been managers who would readily concede a single run for the sake of choking off a rally by making an out at second base. That is, they have refused to take a chance on a close play at home, in order to get a fairly certain out in the middle, an out that would put a sudden stop to the other club's momentum. And sometimes, when there are two runners on who are both convinced the play will be made at the plate, a cutoff and fast throw have produced a double play that ended the threat with that single run.

The cutoff man does not decide on his own when he is to cut off the throw to the plate and try for an out elsewhere. It is up to the catcher, who can see the man trying to score as well as the other runners, to decide where the best chance lies. And the cutoff man acts to intercept the throw only when he hears the catcher yell "Cut it off!" Then he has to know instantly where to throw, whether to hang on to the ball and merely bluff some runner back to the bag, or whether to make no play at all. Other players may shout advice about where to throw, but it is your job to make sure there is someone to take a throw and a chance of putting a runner out.

The first baseman, like every other player in the infield, must be ready to cover any open base and back up throws from the outfield. While the shortstop or second baseman will act more often as relay men, by hustling out on the

grass to get a long throw on a ball hit deep, you have to
get out there if nobody else does. And someone should
always back up the relay man, in case the throw from
the outfielder is off target. Don't wait around on the
theory that this job belongs to somebody else. It's *your*
job if no one else remembers to do it.

The Second Baseman

The liveliest spot on a baseball diamond and the most
exciting place to be — if you like to be moving, hopping,
making tags, taking throws, relaying signs, and getting
into combination plays — is right in the middle, at second
base or shortstop. The defensive strength of any ball club
must always be concentrated right down the middle,
from catcher to shortstop–second base to center field. The
club can afford to give up a little agility and some
defensive skill at the corners (first and third bases) in
return for power at bat. But even a .400 batting average
will not do a team much good if its owner is booting
ground balls, making wild throws, and messing up

strategy in the middle. The great Mickey Mantle started out as a shortstop. He once made five errors in one game, and the club just could not afford to keep him there, despite the fact that he could hit a ball out of the county.

The second baseman is often just as busy as the shortstop with ground balls and double plays and relay throws. But he does not need the throwing strength that a shortstop must have. Still, he has to make fast and difficult throws, and he has to field his position with the same aggressiveness — wanting every ball to be hit in his direction and putting the tag on runners despite their size and speed.

Because batting strategy so often calls for hits to right field — either on a hit-and-run or to move a runner from second to third — the second baseman has a wide area to cover and has many kinds of balls to cope with: line drives, sizzling ground balls, humpbacked drives into the short outfield, infield flies, and often fly balls down the right field line. The advice given the first baseman on fielding grounders goes double to the second baseman and the shortstop: Bend your back and knees. Charge the ball, don't try to round it up. Get your head right over the ball as you field it and watch it right into your glove. Field the ball out in front of your forward foot, in your natural stride. Only on explosive drives that come at you before you have a chance to move in on them do you sometimes have to give ground a little. Then you will step or hop quickly back to gain that split second you need to get your hands in position. This is a move that will become instinctive as you practice.

The most difficult ground ball to field is the one that comes straight at you, making it difficult to judge the hop or the speed of the ball. This is the type of grounder, therefore, that you should practice on the most, even though the ones you have to sprint wide after may look more spectacular. You will find that you can field the straight-at-you balls most quickly by taking them on the short hop, and of course this means smothering them before they have a chance to bounce high or skitter under your glove. You will make a lot of errors on these balls. But don't let that stop you from working on them. The more errors you put behind you, the fewer you will have in your future. And there is no way in the world you can learn to field your position except by actually playing there every chance you get. Don't ever back away from a chance because you think the players are too good for you. Play over your head if you need to, but try to play as often as you find time. In between games, you can have someone hit balls to you on the ground, so you begin to discover all the different things a ground ball can do — and you can begin to make a habit of getting your head right over the ball as you field it.

When a ground ball goes to your right or left, try to cut it off as short as you can. Don't run back and wait for it. Charge right across its path, head down, knees bent, back bent, and smother it right on the ground. The sooner you get to it, the more chance you will have of getting the man out.

It is a good idea to watch every pitch right into the catcher's glove, hoping it will come back to you. Some players like to watch the ball all the way in from the pitcher's hand. Others will keep their eyes fixed on the batter and will pick the ball up as it approaches the plate. I don't believe it matters which way you do it, as long as you have your eye on that ball *before* it reaches the bat.

Your position as you watch the pitch come in should be a crouch — back bent, knees flexed. Some infielders, particularly third basemen, like to crouch so low that

their chests nearly touch their thighs and their hands
dangle to the ground. You need not get down that far
if it is not comfortable, but you should have your hands
and arms free. Shake them every now and then to keep
them loose. And whatever you do, don't get your elbows
between your knees! It is too easy to get locked into that
position for a second or so and be unable to get to the
ball before it gets by. Be sure too that you get your
weight *forward*, on the balls of your feet, so you can get
off to a good fast start. Don't play "on your heels" or you
will never get to field a slow-hit ball on time. And try

to get in front of the ball so your body will stop it. Of course you can't always do this, but you can probably do it more often than you think. It may be a temptation, when the ball is going to your bare-hand side to cross your arm over to glove the ball in fancy style. Far better you avoid the fancy stuff and get into a position where you can stop the ball even on a bad hop. Sometimes, to do this on a ball that is scooting for the grass and going past to your left, you can just jump, spider fashion, to land on both feet right in front of the ball. Of course you can't *always* get in front of a fast-moving ball. But you should always give it a try.

Once in a great while you can stop a ball with a dive, full length, with your glove hand outstretched. But you should do that only in dire emergency, when you know you have a chance to stop the ball. Don't do it just to show the coach, or somebody, how hard you are trying. Once you put yourself on the ground that way, you are out of the play and no use to the team for a few seconds. Never mind about appearances. Do what you have to do to stop the ball. If you can't get it, and it goes on by into the outfield, you can do more good by scrambling to cover the base than you can by putting on a show.

If the ball does get through you, even when you have got your glove on it, scramble right after it. Dog it down! Don't let it get away! Runners are not always going top speed. There may still be a play at some other base. Or you may just be able to get the ball and *still* get off a throw that will nail the runner. Make up your mind you are going to get that ball no matter what it does and keep scrambling until you get it or it is hopelessly past you.

A big advantage of getting your body in front of the ball, besides your chance of stopping the ball and keeping it in front of you, is the chance to get both hands on the ball. Because your job isn't complete until you have that ball solidly in your throwing hand, ready to throw. But you must be mighty sure you have the ball. Watch it right into the glove and grab it there. Sometimes it seems to me that about half the infield errors in amateur ball come from some infielder's trying to throw the ball before he has a good hold on it. So get hold of the ball *first*. Then come up to throw. Is there a player on first to get your throw? If he hasn't got there yet, keep moving toward first, to shorten the throw. Then let him have it, overhand, straight and hard, about shoulder-high.

There are plays of course which do not give you time to straighten up for the throw. A slow-hit ground ball that draws you in on the grass near the pitcher's mound is going to force you to come charging in at top speed, because the runner will be moving faster than the ball. When you field a ball like this you will usually have time only to sling it sidearm, right across the body, to the first baseman. So that is a throw you must practice, even though you will use it only on rare occasions. You should practice throwing underhand too, although that is another type of throw you use only in an emergency.

Sometimes a ground ball — a drag bunt especially — may come almost to a dead stop as you charge it. This sort of ball has to be fielded in the bare hand and slung from the spot you pick it up, in an underhand move. The secret to fielding a ball like this successfully is to run, not straight at it but to the left side, so that you will pick it up as you go by. But you must be extra careful on this play to keep your eye on the ball every second, right until you have it firmly in your grasp. If you try to snag it as you look toward first to see the runner, you'll be very likely to leave it lying there, all shiny and white, right in the grass behind you.

Because slow-hit ground balls and drag bunts have to be fielded promptly to beat the runner, it is a good idea to sneak in a little closer to the plate when you have a man at bat who likes to try this maneuver. Of course a bunt near the foul line will be fielded by the first baseman, who will be charging the plate, close to the line, to keep the ball from getting by to his left. And the pitcher may be running in too when a bunt is expected. Then it is up to the second baseman to cover first base, standing at the inside corner with his toe in contact with the base and his hands held chest-high to give the target — inside the baseline.

The second baseman and the shortstop both act at different times as pivot man on a double play, depending on which man has to field the ball. Sometimes the man who fields the ball makes the play close enough to the bag so that he can tag the base for the first put-out, too. Usually the shortstop is in a better position to do this, and the second baseman will do best on almost every occasion when he fields the ball to let the shortstop make the put-out. Your throw to him, when you field a ball close to the bag, should be an underhand toss. Move toward him as you make the toss — and let him *see* the ball! Hold it in your bare hand, with your glove well out of the way, and try to get it to him when he is still two or three steps from the base. Give it to him shoulder-high so he can get his throw off fast.

When you have a runner on first, with a good chance for a double play, you can edge a few steps closer to the bag, so that you will be able to beat the runner to it in plenty of time. Of course you must stay alert for a ball that goes to your left, and you must have an understanding with your shortstop as to which of you will cover second base in the event of an attempted steal. Ordinarily, when there is a left-handed batter up, the shortstop will cover, and you will take over when the batter is right-handed. But you want to make sure, by exchanging some sort of signal (or even getting together and talking about it), just who has the responsibility.

It must be granted that double plays in amateur ball are often a lost cause, because the fielders are not often swift enough and strong-armed enough to get to the bases on time and get off accurate throws in a hurry. Unless you can really see a double play staring you in the face, you should go for the out at first base. Better one sure out than two doubtful.

All the same, when you *can* make a double play, you should know how you are going to do it. I don't believe that you should try to do it big-league style unless you have played a lot of baseball and really have hopes of becoming a professional player. Frank Crosetti, who coached the New York Yankees for many years, always believed that amateur players should make a double play in a safe manner, avoiding a collision with the runner and the leap into the air the big-league pivot man sometimes has to perform. There is no reason why kids who are playing for fun should get into a knock-down contest to make a put-out at second.

When you are playing pivot man on a double play — that is, when the shortstop or some other player has fielded the ball and you are going to take the throw — you have to scramble for the base. But you do not want to be standing there without the ball, waiting for the throw, and you do not want to be moving so fast you will keep on going past the base. So the thing to do is start *fast* for the base, in good long strides, then, if the ball is not thrown to you before you get there, shorten your stride quickly, the way you do when you see a fence in front of you, and move into the base with your eye on the ball. When you get the ball, tag the base on the outfield side and push off — *backwards* — to get out of the runner's path. From outside the baseline, turn and face first base and throw hard to the baseman, shoulder-high, stepping toward first base as you throw. This will not be the sort of lightning play you see in the big leagues. But you don't have to deal with big-league baserunning, either.

When you field the ball and the shortstop is the pivot man, the throw to the base is sometimes a problem. If you get the ball near the base, it is best to let the shortstop make the force play, unless you are practically on the base when you field the ball. Because he has the runner in view and is facing first base, he can more easily avoid the runner while making the force-out and get off a faster throw to first.

In the bad old days, veteran big leaguers used to haze rookie infielders by delaying their throws so the rookie had to stand "in the pivot" until the runner was right on top of him and would come barreling into him as he took the throw. Don't you do that to your teammates!

If you field the ball well down the baseline and you have a pretty certain double play, you will have a difficult throw to make, because you will have to swing back to your right to get proper leverage for a right-handed throw. If you are agile and practice the move often, you may be able to snap the throw off flat-footed, by pivoting on the balls of your feet to twist your body well to the right. When you make this move, your left knee will almost touch the ground. But because the throw is a short one, you will probably have all the leverage you need to put real snap into the throw and get it to the shortstop chest-high while he is still on the other side of the base.

On a steal, when you cover the base, you should straddle the bag, facing first base, as you await the throw. *Stay there*, even if you see the throw is going to hit the dirt. Do not try to make it a good throw by going to meet it. It is up to you to make the low throws look good. But if the throw is well off the base, or far over your head, you will have to forget the runner and try to keep the ball from going through.

Do not put the ball down to tag the runner until you see which side of the base he is coming on. Sometimes, if you get the ball down too early, the runner can study it a while and may even be able to kick it right out of

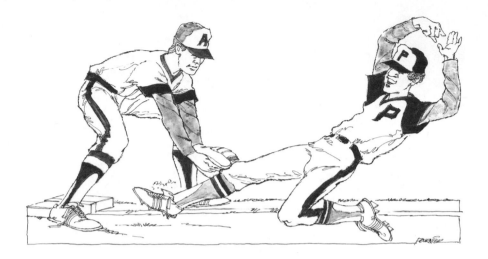

your glove as he slides in. So hold the ball in both hands as he approaches, then stick it down quickly between him and the base. You make the tag with both hands, and with the *back* of your gloved hand toward the runner. The inside of your wrist is more tender than the back and can be scratched or gouged more easily. Play safe by always turning the tough side toward the runner's sliding feet.

Sometimes, even in amateur ball, a double steal may be attempted and when that happens, you may be able to take advantage of it and louse up the strategy completely. You can do this if you have good peripheral vision — the ability to see out of the corners of your eyes — and can move fast and throw hard. The purpose of a double steal is to force a throw to second base that will allow a runner to score from third. The runner starts down from first base with the pitch, and the runner on third base takes as good a lead as he can get, watching the catcher all the time. As soon as the catcher lets the throw go to second, the runner on third digs full speed for home.

What the infielder does on this play is keep half an eye on the runner on third, even as he is racing in to take the throw. Of course he has to center his main attention on the ball, but he can still stay alive to what the runner is doing, if he is good at picking up moves with the corner of his eye. If the runner breaks, then you should run in to meet the throw from the catcher to take it right behind the pitcher's mound and fire it back fast and hard. It is a beautiful play when it works and can set the whole club rejoicing. But it takes two good arms to make it work — one on the catcher and one on the infielder — plus a pair of fast feet and sharp eyes. Amateur teams are not always blessed that way. But they can sometimes get the same result if the catcher learns to make a convincing bluff of a throw to second — a real, all-out, hard throw from well behind his shoulder, except that he *keeps* the ball. Such a move often nails the runner from third far down the baseline, where he can't scramble back.

The second baseman, like the shortstop, often has to range into the outfield to take short fly balls. Flies over first base, down the foul line, are often much easier for the second baseman to catch than for the first baseman, who will be backing up under them or trying to get them over his shoulder. A fast second baseman can cover a fair amount of short right field and make outs on foul balls well over the line. On all catches of this sort, you should be doubly aware of what runners you have on base and how many are out. With less than two out, a base runner can advance on a caught fly, fair or foul, and you must take care, especially if there is a runner on third, not to get yourself hung up into a position where you can't throw.

When you go into the outfield for a fly ball, make sure the outfielder knows you are after it. Yell loud and constantly that you've got it. But yelling is not enough. You must keep waving your hands over your head, motioning everyone to stay clear. Of course if the outfielder warns you off, you have to give way to him. But stand by just in case the ball pops out of his glove.

The really difficult fly balls are those that go right over your head. The immediate temptation on these is to try to backpedal fast enough to get under them. But you often can't do this. Too many times you will get your feet tangled and go down on your fanny. It is just as difficult to catch them while running back and simultaneously looking over your shoulder. You have very little room, must keep twisting and turning, and usually have a hard time keeping on your feet. The best way is to size the fly up quickly and pick out the spot behind you where you figure the ball will drop. Run to that spot. *Then* look up to the ball. Maybe you'll be too far off, but you'll probably be reasonably close and should be able to make the play easily. When the ball is right over your head as you run away from the diamond and seems to be coming down right in front of you, you will usually find it is moving *away* from you. You will probably have to reach out farther than you think. So be ready to lunge for the ball, because it will not be dropping straight.

Every ballplayer has trouble with fly balls in bright

sun or high wind. If you have sunglasses, as you should have, put in some time learning to flip them down quickly. Few things are more foolish looking on a diamond than a ballplayer who cannot get his sunglasses down. Try to get so you can make the flip in a split second.

But sunglasses or not, don't ever look right *into* the sun for the ball. Get an angle on it if you can so you can look up sideways, using your gloved hand to shade your eyes. Perhaps you can at least get glimpse enough to line the ball up, and if you do lose it in the sun, you will have an idea where it is going to fall. *Never* give up on it! At least get your glove up in the general area and take a chance on getting it. It may show up suddenly, so you can make a quick stab.

In trying for a windblown fly ball, try to make the wind bring the ball to you. That is, get past the spot where it seems headed and if the wind carries it, let it be in your direction. If you are playing in a park with high stands, you will usually find that a windy day causes a strong draft *away* from the stands, that will blow balls back to you when they seem out of play. So don't give up on them too soon.

The best way to catch a fly ball is reasonably high, so your hands will be in a position to throw and so that, if the ball does pop out (and infield flies often have excessive spin), you will have another chance to grab it before it hits the ground.

The second-base position probably requires more practice than any other, because the throws are so varied and there is so much area to cover. You have to range all the way to first base — covering first sometimes if pitcher and first baseman are converging on a bunt — into right field, *behind* second base on balls hit up the middle, and all the area between second and first. Most of the time you will probably play nearly halfway to first, closing in on second base a little when there is a runner on first who is likely to be running on the pitch. With three and two on the batter, he is likely to be running. With three and two with two out, he is sure to be running.

But the most difficult chance and the one you will probably see the most of in amateur play is the slow roller almost straight at you. Sometimes this type of ball, having been badly topped, is moving about half the speed of the runner. So you *must* charge such balls and not wait for them. And, as I said, you have to snap your throw right across your chest after you have fielded the ball. Of course it is always best to face the bag and throw overhand, stepping toward the bag as you throw, but on these slow rollers there just isn't time. So you will make yourself into a good second baseman if you can perfect this throw. You will also get such a kick out of it that you will wish for many slow rollers and drag bunts to come your way.

There is one more fielding play I have not mentioned: the ground ball you field close to first base, when the play is at second. On this ball, the best way to throw is to let the natural swing of your body as you field the ball carry you all the way around to the left, so you wind up facing second base. Then you throw overhand, moving toward the base as you throw. On this somewhat longer throw, you make up for the delay of the throw by the extra speed behind it.

The best throw you will have to make is probably the one you will make to third when you act as relay man. Here again, you have to get out on the grass, waving your hands so the outfielder can pick you up quickly. But you do not turn your back on the diamond. Instead

you stand so that you can keep one eye on the runner.
You will probably be going for the lead runner, if the
game is close. But you want to know where all the
runners are, so you will not have to search them out after
you have the ball.

The basic system of the relay is for the outfielder to
make a long throw and for you to make a short throw,
because yours has to be right on target, usually right on
the base, where the catcher or baseman can make the
tag. You will want to receive that throw high enough
so you can get your own throw off in a hurry. If the
outfielder's throw is weak, however, and is going to fall
short, don't wait. Go out to meet it so you can catch it
at good height. Knowing then approximately where the
runners are, look quickly at the lead runner and decide
in a flash whether you have a chance to get him. Don't
bluff a throw! If you can't get him, go for the other
runner, at second or third. You have got to *know* where
those runners are going to be, and if you have kept one
eye on them as the play developed, you won't waste time
looking for them. The throw to third should be low,
right at the base and inside the line, unless it is a force

play, when it should be shoulder-high. It goes without saying that you first make sure there is someone to take the throw.

Occasionally the second baseman will act as cutoff man, although that job is usually left to the first baseman or shortstop, depending on what field the ball goes to. The cutoff man, as I said, plays inside the diamond where he can keep all the bases in view. The outfielder, throwing to home plate, is supposed to fire the ball in a low enough trajectory so the cutoff man can reach it if need be. And the catcher is supposed to shout "Cut it off" or "Let it go" depending on how he sizes up the chance to make a play at home. But the cutoff man can act on his own — if, for instance, the run about to score is not a crucial one and he sees an excellent chance to shoot down a runner at another base. When you are going to cut off the throw, you need not stand waiting for it. Go to meet it, with your mind made up where you are going to throw — and throw the ball fast, as soon as you know there is someone there to take it. And remember: Always look to see if there is a fielder to take the throw, no matter how many voices are telling you to throw to this base or that. The final judgment is yours.

Infielders always back each other up. When one fielder goes out to act as relay man, another should get in place, about twenty-five feet behind, to back up the throw. If no one else has done it, *you* do it. And always expect the throw to get by the relay man and come to you, so *you* keep track of the runners too.

The second baseman should make a habit of backing up the throw that comes from the catcher to the pitcher any time there is a runner on base. That throw, it is true, seldom gets by the pitcher. But sometimes it does, especially in amateur ball, and it can be disastrous if no one is there to keep it from trickling on through to the outfield.

You may have to face the fact that your arm has not developed its full power and you may not be able to zip the ball, say, from short right field to third base with as much speed as you would like. If you know the throw is too long for you, don't send a looping throw. Instead, take a few quick steps toward the base, then throw. The best way to move, so as to keep your left foot forward and pointing at the base all the time, is a sort of skipping hop, like a dance step or a boxer's move, with the left foot always forward. Or if you are far out of your range, you can sprint toward the base and let the throw go as you are moving. This movement toward the target will give enough extra impetus to make up a little of what you lose by the delay. And it is far more fun to be able to power the ball straight and true than to try to loft it to a target.

When there is a runner on second base, the second baseman has to be concerned with keeping him close. It is almost impossible for a second baseman to pick off a runner there, unless the runner really goofs off, for the second baseman is always in the runner's line of sight. But runners do goof off at times and if you have an alert, strong-armed catcher, you may be able to catch a runner who has advanced too far with the pitch. Usually, however, all you can do is help scare him back when he takes too big a lead. You do that by bluffing a dash for the base. Keep going until he shortens his lead. Pickoffs are usually performed by the shortstop, who is out of the runner's view and can thus sneak in close without being noticed.

When you have to cover first base on plays that draw the first baseman into the diamond, remember to leave most of the base for the runner as you take the throw.

Reach toward the throw to get it sooner. But leave the base and go after the ball if it's way off target.

Infielders sometimes think they must stay out of the runner's way at all costs, on the theory that "the baseline belongs to the runner." But that is not always true. If you are making a legitimate effort to field a ball, the runner must avoid you or be called out for interference. And on the run to first the runner must *stay off* the baseline and run outside it.

The Shortstop

The shortstop, who usually plays the deepest of all infielders and has the widest range, is also in a position to have the most fun. He has a base to cover and short outfield in which to catch fair and foul flies, has to go clear to the left field fence after fouls many times, must be ready to move in on the grass for slow ground balls, starts most double plays, ranges deep into the "hole" near third base for hot ground balls, spears line drives, relays throws, and picks off runners. He has to be the best fielder on the club, with one of the strongest and quickest arms, able to throw off balance, underhand, sidearm, or just sling the ball without taking time to cock his arm.

If you are going to play this position and enjoy it, you will have to play lots and lots of baseball and be able to play close to the ground, with back and knees bent and hands, wrists, and arms all loose and supple. You must practice with every kind of ground ball, actually be a hog for practice, so you can learn to charge the ball fast or slow, adjusting your approach to reach the ball on the short hop and smother it. The shortstop, playing right in the midst of things, close to the pitcher and the third and second basemen, is often the sparkplug of the team. He shouts encouragement to pitcher and infield, helps to slow the pitcher down or helps him get settled after a bad spell, and on some clubs will relay the catcher's signals to the outfield, so the fielders can be ready to move in one direction or another, depending on whether a fast ball or a curve is coming.

Good shortstops, because they have so much experience with ground balls of every type, do so much tagging of runners, and relay so many throws, can usually play any position in the infield. So they play a lot more baseball than anyone else on the club.

If you want to play short, you have to be right-handed. You must have a strong arm, be fast on your feet, and be able to get off accurate throws even when off balance. So make up your mind, when you choose this position, that you are going to take every chance that is granted you to play baseball. Horn into every sort of ball game where there is room, no matter how fast the company. If the other players are better than you are, you will learn to improve. If they are below your caliber, you can play all over the field.

The shortstop fields ground balls, of course, just as the second baseman does, with back bent and knees bent, arms free, and hands out front. No doubt you will make a lot of errors. Just call them money in the bank. Go after the impossible ground balls. Sure, you'll boot most of them. But before long you'll be coming up with some the other guys wouldn't even try for. When you get a chance for infield practice, ask to have balls driven hard, straight at you. These are always the tough ones and it takes more than the ordinary amount of practice to learn to judge these so you can, as the big leaguers say, "make your hop" — that is, charge the ball at just the right pace to reach it on the short hop before it has a chance to scoot off erratically or bounce over your head.

Your arm has to have the power of a pitcher's arm to make that long throw from the "hole" to first base. As a matter of fact, you probably won't be able to power the ball that distance until after you have been playing for several seasons. All throws from deep in your position may be difficult for a while. But you can shorten them in the manner recommended to the second baseman — by taking that skipping hop or "boxer's shuffle" toward first base before you uncork the straight overhand throw. Just keep your left toe pointed toward first base and face the base directly, and move toward the base as you throw. Better to get where you can bang that ball *hard* than to try to loft it over to the base.

Every ground ball you have a chance of reaching belongs to you, whether it was something too hot for the third baseman to handle or a ball too far to his right for the second baseman to reach. The wider the range you cover the more valuable you are, and the more fun you will have.

There will be many times when you have to run so far to grab a ground ball that you will *have* to throw it while off balance, perhaps just slinging it from the spot where you picked it up, with your body still bent over and your weight all forward. If you keep your eye right on the first baseman's glove when you make this throw, you will have a good chance of making it accurate. But don't look to the base until *after* you have a firm hold of the ball. Keep your eye right on that ball and your head down until you see it in your glove. You can practice this throw by setting baseballs on the ground and trying to field them on the dead run. Or have someone roll them toward you when you are far enough away that you have to take half a dozen good long strides to get to the ball. Have someone playing first to whom you can throw. And maybe you'd better have someone else to chase the throws that get by him.

When the second baseman is playing pivot on a double play, or on a force-out at second when that seems an easier out than getting the runner at first, you have to perform just the way we recommended that the second baseman complete the play when the shortstop is pivot, except that your throw will never be so difficult as some of his. If you toss the ball, be sure you let him see it. Once in a hundred times the *only* way you can beat the runner is to flip the ball out of your glove after a one-hand stab. But never do that if you can avoid it. Too often it makes for a bad error by the second baseman, who cannot see the ball until it is on top of him.

When you throw the ball to the pivot man, try to give it to him at throwing height, about at the letters, just as you want to get it from him. Be sure he sees it coming (he may be looking at the runner) and let him have it before he gets to the base.

The shortstop will usually act as relay man on drives to left or center field, because it is not good policy to let the third baseman leave his base unguarded. And the shortstop will frequently be cutoff man on throws to the plate. He also has the job of covering third base when the third baseman goes in for a bunt, or when the third baseman is acting as cutoff man on a throw from the outfield. Often the shortstop, by scurrying over to cover when the third baseman is cutting off the throw, can make a crucial tag-out at third.

When the shortstop is the pivot on a double play, he

goes right across the base, taking the throw before he gets there, dragging his toe across the base to make the out and then making the throw to first from outside the baseline. The job is easier for him because he will have the runner in view all the time, will be facing first base to some degree as he moves, and will be able to see the runner headed for first.

For the same reason — his better position — the short-stop should try to get as many ground balls as he can that go to his left, especially those that go right up the middle. Sometimes the second baseman can reach these, but even if he does, he is headed away from first base and has to stop and turn to make the throw, while the shortstop can just keep right on going, with just a slight change in direction, and get his throw off while moving toward the target — always an advantage. If the ball is not hit too hard, the shortstop can sometimes get a ground ball that goes to the other side of second base, and if he can, he should.

A tricky ball to deal with is the chopper that bounds over the pitcher's head, traveling slowly over second base. You have to charge this ball with all your might, because it gives the runner too much time to reach base if you wait for the ball. You have to sprint right in after it to grab it behind the mound if you can and then whip the ball over without straightening up. The fact that you must make these desperation throws on some plays, how-ever, should not prompt you to forget the basic fact that it is always better to straighten up and throw overhand if you have time.

The shortstop has to work things out with the men on either side of him — who will do what under certain circumstances, and what play is in the making. Because the shortstop can always see the catcher's signals, he always knows when a curve ball or a fast ball or a change-up is coming and he can pass the word to his mates. A right-handed batter is likely to slam a change-up pitch or an inside pitch, right along the left field line, and the third baseman will be able to sneak a little closer to the line if he knows one of these is coming. Of course he should not move too soon, or the batter may pick up the news. But he can edge over as soon as the pitch is made — provided he knows what's coming. An outside pitch to a right-handed batter may mean a ground ball to right, and the second baseman will want to be ready for that. Signals can be simple voice signals that sound like ordinary "talk-it-up" chatter that goes on in the infield all the time.

The depth of your position at shortstop will depend on the strength of your own arm and the quality of the opposition. Not too many amateur players can drive a ball through the infield with full power, so you need not try to imitate some big-league hero in playing out near the grass. Don't get so far back that you cannot complete a throw to first without a bounce. Of course you can always move toward your target to shorten the throw. But it is better if you can shorten it by charging the ball and taking it in close.

The shortstop is the key to the pickoff play at second base. He can give the pitcher a signal for it or, better still, he can just have an understanding with the catcher to give the signal or with the pitcher to start the count just as soon as he sees the shortstop is closer to the base than the runner is. To perfect this play the shortstop and pitcher should practice counting in the same rhythm — one-a-two-a-three. At the count of two the shortstop breaks for the base and at the count of three the pitcher turns and throws to the base. This is a nifty play and an easy one to perfect, even on the sandlots. The only trouble is that sometimes it works so niftily that even the umpire is caught napping and misses the call completely. (It happened in the 1950 World Series when everybody in the park, including the runner, knew the runner was out. But the umpire, who was taken completely by surprise, called him safe.) It is sometimes called the "daylight" play because a pitcher will know it is on as soon as he can see daylight between the shortstop and the runner — with the shortstop of course closer to second base than the runner is.

If you cannot get closer to the bag than the runner is, you can at least keep him from getting too big a lead by bluffing a run to the bag every now and then, scuffing the gravel so he will hear your movement. And you should break for the bag after the pitch, because most runners will habitually move several strides down the baseline with the pitch and sometimes one of them may get careless about hustling back. If you have one of those strollers who likes to dance ahead on the pitch and then take his time about getting back, a sudden dash for the bag may give the catcher a chance to snap a throw down to pick him off.

The Third Baseman

A third baseman does not need to cover as much ground as the players to his left, but he must have quick reflexes and lots of agility. It is good too if he has a powerful arm. But if his arm is not unusually strong, he should at least practice getting rid of the ball fast. He should put in a lot of practice at picking up baseballs, getting into throwing position with a quick hop — right foot back, left foot pointed at first base — and letting fly with a minimum of wasted motion. It is a long, long throw from third to first, and there is no time to adjust your grip on the ball or crank up your arm. Even if you don't possess all the speed in the world in your arm, you can beat the runner often if you can "release" the ball in a hurry.

Sometimes, when you are first starting to play, you may have to take those skip-hops toward first base to get within range. And because runners in amateur ball are not all fast starters (a lot of them like to look and see where the ball is going) or real speed demons on the baseline, you can still beat them with a strong throw, even if you have to move closer before you let the ball go.

While the third baseman will of course field ground balls as the other fielders do — aggressively, trying to take them on the short hop — he gets more than the usual number of red-hot drives that give him no chance to do much more than get himself in front of the ball. Because these drives come so fast, it is often possible to knock them down, pick them up, and still get the runner at first base. You just have to take care not to dodge those hits, or try to sidestep and glove them blindly. If you keep the ball in front of you, even if you cannot field it cleanly, you will have a good chance of making the out.

A third baseman cannot afford to play too deep because his position is too vulnerable to bunts. A good bunter who sees a third baseman well behind the base-line or playing "on his heels" — that is, with his weight centered in his tail and his body almost straight up — counts that as practically a free ticket to first base, because he knows the player cannot get the sort of start needed to field a well-placed bunt in time.

You will see most big-league third basemen go into

an exaggerated crouch every time the pitcher addresses
the plate — body bent almost double, eyes intent on the
batter, hands almost touching the ground, weight on the
balls of their feet. That is so they can pounce forward
the instant the batter gets into bunting position. It is
good practice to move forward a few steps with the pitch,
unless of course you have a runner on third that you
have to hold reasonably close. When the situation calls
for a bunt, you should be playing inside the baseline,
poised to dart forward as soon as the pitch is on its way.
Even when a bunt is not in order, you ought not to play
much more than two or three strides behind the baseline
between second and third.

Every ball that goes on the ground to your left is yours

to try for. There is no such thing as letting it go to the shortstop unless he shouts you off it. Whatever you can reach you should field, because you can get the ball so much more quickly.

In late innings of close ball games, you will want to play close to the foul line, so that nothing can get past you to your right. Anything that goes through there is an almost certain extra-base hit and you cannot afford those. Get your glove on the ball and you can at least hold it to a single.

A third baseman has to field bunts with lightning speed, because the long throw gives him far less time to make the out than is granted to the first baseman, when a bunt goes down the first baseline. So the third baseman will have to make more off-balance throws than any other fielder and will often have to snatch up a ball in his bare hand and sling it across the diamond without straightening up. That is a move that you must practice and practice and practice. It is not the sort of throw you want to make for kicks, although it must be allowed that it is a thrill to make such a play successfully. When the ball gets to you quickly, of course you want to straighten up and throw overhand. Those off-balance, underhand slings have too great a percentage of error, and are strictly for moments of desperation. It just happens that the third baseman faces a lot of desperate moments!

If a bunt is right on the baseline, the right play is to let it roll foul, if it will, and then to brush it off quickly, away from the baseline, once it gets into foul territory. (Don't "brush it away" when it is still fair, or your teammates may lynch you!) But if it is on the grass and rolling to a stop, you have to *run by it*, and pick it up with the bare hand as you go by. The temptation here is always to lift your head and look at first base or at the runner just a split second before you have the ball in your hand. Most often when you do that, you pick up nothing but a handful of air or a blade of grass. Train yourself to concentrate on that ball and not to lift your eyes from it until you have it clutched tightly in your throwing hand. *Then* you sight your target and let fly. And remember: Don't run straight at the ball, or you'll get tangled up with yourself when you try to pick it up. Run to the *left* of the ball, so you can scoop it up easily in your bare hand.

The third baseman has special problems with a runner on third. There are not too many pickoffs at third base but you still must keep the runner close and be ready to nail him if he gets careless. So you cannot play too far off the base, and you must remind the pitcher that there is a runner there, because pitchers sometimes forget the runner at third. It is true that not many runners steal home these days. But that does not mean it can never happen.

The runner on third will usually run a few steps up the baseline with the pitch. Once the pitch goes past the batter, and you have a runner on third, you should dash back to the base, to give the catcher a chance to throw down there to pick off a careless runner.

With a runner on third, you have to have an understanding with both pitcher and shortstop about how to play a bunt. It is best in these circumstances if the pitcher can field the ball. But if it comes to you, you have got to field it, regardless, and *somebody* must be ready to cover third. Also, when a batter hits a sacrifice fly to score a runner from third base, you and the shortstop must agree when the shortstop is to be covering the base. On a sacrifice fly, you should get yourself off into foul territory behind the base and keep your eye on the runner to make sure he does not leave the base before the fly is caught.

In amateur ball, with amateur umpires, it is a good idea to make sure the umpire also pays close attention. You can help him keep track by pointing to the runner and telling the umpire to watch him, to make sure he does not start too soon. Keep insisting on this. And if the runner does take his foot from the base before the ball makes contact with the fielder's glove, yell a protest *immediately!* Don't wait to see how the play comes out. The umpire may be having doubts about the play, and if you protest at the start, you can help him make up his mind. To holler after the run has scored is not nearly so convincing.

If the fly ball is hit to left field, your position should still be in foul territory, but down the baseline a good way, so you can keep both fielder and runner in view. It the throw comes in fast, the runner may decide to scramble back to third, and you are then in an excellent position to cut off the throw and snap it to the covering shortstop. Only you have to be sure that the shortstop is aware of his duty on this play. Talk about it before the play develops.

Some third basemen, as they scramble back to the base to take a throw from another infielder, forget to keep close track of where the ball went. That is why a third baseman must be extra alert. He has to know the position of the runners and keep an eye too on the ball, as he is in the process of getting back to the base. It is important to know just where the ball is coming from.

On a tag play at third, the third baseman has got to hold his ground without flinching. The runner may come sliding in hard, and even come fast enough to overslide the base. You must straddle the base and *wait* for the throw, figuring it is going to be a bad throw. Reach for it when it comes, or dig it out of the dirt, but don't leave the base to meet it unless it is clearly well off target. Put on the tag with both hands, with the *back* of the glove to the runner.

And even when the out is made at third, you must be aware of what play comes next. There is often another play following an out at third. You must be figuring what it will be even before you make the out. Once you've done that, be ready to throw again. If there was a runner on first, then there may still be a force play at second that a quick throw will complete. Or the batter may be trying to take an extra base on the throw. Be ready for either of these possibilities. Act fast! And throw hard!

While the third baseman, like all the infielders, has to be ready to back up throws of every sort and may sometimes be backup man on a relay from the outfield, he should be much more careful about leaving his base unguarded. There is no one on the other side to take the base if he leaves it, so he should never wander so far that he cannot beat a runner to the bag.

On a squeeze bunt, if the third baseman fields the ball it is just about impossible to catch the man at home, unless it has been a safety squeeze (on which the runner does not come in until after the ball is bunted) and the runner is a bit slow. Don't make a useless throw on this play. Get hold of the ball and *look* to see where the other runners, if any, may be. Sometimes, if a third baseman gets careless, *two* men may score on the play, provided the runner at second got a good start. If no other runner threatens, then get the ball to first hard and fast.

High foul balls behind third base are best left to the shortstop, who can get a better angle on them. But fouls between third and home are in your range. If they are close to third, it is better you take them for your glove is better suited to catching fly balls than is the catcher's. Don't go if you are called off, and make sure the catcher knows you are taking the ball. Yell and wave your arms. A collision with a big catcher who is wearing all his equipment is something you may remember the rest of the season.

The Outfielders

There have been outfielders, even in the big leagues, who have made their jobs the easiest on the club, who have spent most of their glove time dreaming of their next trip to bat or trying to get news from the scoreboard about what other hitters were doing. But most of such players had very short careers, some lasting only long enough for the pitchers to catch on to their batting weaknesses, some fading as soon as they stopped hitting the ball into the seats. Or else they became designated hitters and spent a lot of time on the bench.

It is true that anyone who has played considerable

baseball can catch balls on the fly without much difficulty. But there is far more to being a good outfielder than just catching fly balls. An outfielder has to move. He has to know where the batter is likely to hit the ball. He has to be able to throw and has to know where and when to throw. He has to learn to work with his teammates to make the outs.

If you are going to play the outfield, you have to learn first of all to run on your toes. Running on your heels will make your eyes blur while you are moving and make it difficult to gauge the flight of the ball you are trying to catch. Practice running every chance you get and practice running on your toes. Stay on your toes going upstairs. Trot downstairs on your toes.

Then you need to judge the flight of a ball when it is coming off the bat, especially if you're in center field. That is a lot harder than it seems. A ball that seems to be streaking right at you will sometimes drop like a tired bird and plop into the sod yards in front of you. Or what looks like a soft line drive may seem to take wings without any warning and rise and rise as it gets near you so that it sails far over your head. Nothing in the world will teach you how to judge the flight of a ball except practice.

And more practice. And some extra practice besides.

One of the greatest outfielders in the history of major-league baseball was Tris Speaker, who played in Boston and Cleveland when the century was very young. He played in the days when the outfielder wore a tiny little glove in which each finger came right to the end, and when fielders used to cut out the palms of their gloves so the fly balls would stick there better. No one since, according to the old-timers, has ever done better than Tris in judging the flight of a ball. He was so skilled at it that he could play right behind second base and still get started fast enough to take long fly balls over his shoulder out by the fence.

He developed this skill with the help of a patient teammate who used to come to the park with Tris in the early morning and spend hours hitting fungoes to him. Tris gradually learned that he could tell by the sound of the bat meeting the ball whether it was going to loop up into the air, from having been undercut, or go streaking to the outfield, from having been hit solidly with the "good wood" — the thick part of the bat.

It is also possible, with practice, to recognize from the speed with which the ball travels whether it is going to dip down or go sailing beyond you. But no one can explain these points to you so you can use them. Nothing will ever teach you except catching hundreds of fly balls, and missing hundreds more. Even better than catching fungoes is playing the outfield during batting practice, because a pitched ball hit by a bat acts differently from a ball tossed up by the batter and hit.

Just how you catch the ball is not too important. It is better to take the ball high, near the shoulder, because that puts you into position to throw more quickly and if the ball chances to pop out, you may get an extra stab at it. But many great outfielders have found it comfortable to catch flies waist-high. And one famous showboat used to take them right over the button of his cap. Catch them in the manner that makes you most confident of hanging on to them.

An outfielder, unlike an infielder, has room enough to chase a fly while watching it over his shoulder. Often, with confidence and determination, it is possible to make "impossible" catches this way. If you make up your mind you are going to catch the ball and start off top speed with your eye on the ball, you can be right on the spot when it comes within reach. You do not need to watch your footing. You will have looked the outfield over ahead of time and should know where every minor obstacle may lie. There should not be any serious enough to cause you to take your eye off the ball. Even when it seems you have failed to catch up with it, give it a try! Make a final lunge to get your glove out just as far as your speed and strength will allow. You may just discover the ball nestled there at the very tip of the glove. Sometimes the ball will seem to light there gently as a bird, for you will be traveling in the same direction at the same speed and there will be very little impact. Even if you fail to hold the ball you may tip it into the air high enough to get one more chance at it, or you may even be able to slap it off in the direction of a teammate.

And if the ball does fall beyond you, keep after it. Every portion of a second that is lost in retrieving the ball means more feet of baseline gained by the runner.

Of course, before you ever retrieve the ball, you must *know* exactly what you are going to do with it. If it is far, far out by the fence, you will be looking for a relay man to throw to. He will be out on the grass, waving his hands over his head. Fire the ball straight at him, to reach him shoulder-high. If he is too far beyond your range, charge in a few steps and let the ball go with the full strength and full length of your arm. You can afford to reach back to get your full power into the throw the way a pitcher does. And your momentum, as you move toward the diamond, will be transferred to the ball. Don't loft the ball for distance. Throw hard!

When you field a batted ball within range of the diamond, you will almost invariably be throwing ahead of the lead runner. Or if there are no runners other than the man who hit the ball, you will be throwing to second base. This throw should be planned to hit the ground in front of the infielder and reach him on the bounce, so that there will be no danger of an overthrow that could give extra bases to the runner. Once in a decade an outfielder will show up with an arm so strong and so accurate that he can throw *behind* the runner — in case the runner has made a big turn around first but is not really digging for second. But that is not the play to plan on. Throwing behind the runner could get you kicked out of the outfielder's union, if there were such a thing. It can make a manager or a coach shout bad names at you.

When you field a ball with a man in scoring position, or when you catch a sacrifice fly with a man on third, your throw must go home. But the idea is not to get it home at all cost, by sending it up in a tremendous arc, high over the diamond. It has got to come in straight and low, so it can be hauled down by the cutoff man if the play at home is a lost cause. If your arm is not equal to throwing the full distance, then give the ball to the cutoff man, shoulder-high and with lots of steam on it. When you play this way you will at least have the satisfaction of giving your throwing arm the workout it needs to develop its full strength.

It used to be considered a sin for an outfielder to field a ground ball in any way except by going on one knee in front of it to keep it from getting by. That is still the best way to field a ball that comes to you near the full depth of your position, because there is no one behind you then. But *every* ground ball should be charged. The runner has a full head of steam by the time the ball reaches the outfield and any delay may mean extra bases. So charge right at the ball when you see it hit the sod. If it comes in short, so that your mates have plenty of room to back you up, field it in stride, as an infielder would, with back bent, knees bent, head right over the ball and hands out front. You can make your throw then while you are moving toward the target. Just be sure you *know* ahead of time where you want to throw it and be sure someone is there to receive your throw. Throw with full arm, drawing it well back and giving it all the beef you possess, not for distance so much as for speed. You may have to take a couple of skipping hops to get your weight on your back foot and your full arm into the throw.

Sun and wind give the outfielders more trouble than they do infielders, because a strong wind can carry a high fly a long, long way, and the sun, in the late summer, can stare at you steadily right over the roof of the stands and require sunglasses on every ball that comes your way. But you handle these matters just as the infielders do — never giving up to the sun, trying to get a sidelong glimpse of the ball while you avoid looking right into the sun. Even if you lose it completely, if you have managed to get somewhere near its landing point, you can always stick a glove up and may even get hold of it.

As for the wind, try to make that work for you. On a gusty day you have to keep testing the wind by tossing bits of dust or grass up to see which way it is blowing. Then you make allowances for the wind as you go after a ball, and try if you can to get where the wind will bring the ball to you.

Center field is the most demanding position in the field because the center fielder really has first call on everything and should poach freely on the other fielders' turf if he can line up a ball quickly. He does not have to make the sudden stops the other fielders do because he does not have foul line fences to contend with, although even on the sandlots there are sometimes blows that carry out to the center field walls, and the center fielder has to be aware of how close he is to such obstacles. Most fields in organized leagues have warning tracks around the field so the outfielders can tell, by the feel of cinders under their feet, that they are close to the wall. But not all amateur ball games are played in parks so outfitted. It is a good idea then to take a good look at the fences and the footing in the park you are going to play in. If there is a high wire fence, you will want to avoid getting your face in contact with it and you will want to slam a baseball against it to see what kind of bounce it gives. You also want to pick out some landmarks that will warn you when the fence is close.

Outfielders have to talk to each other continually, so

that each man will know what the other is going to do and everybody will stay awake to how many outs have been made, what sort of hitter is coming up, and where the throw should go. When you have lined up a fly ball, unless it is clearly in your own turf, make sure the other fielders know you are going for it. Keep yelling "I've got it!" as you move after the ball. But if the center fielder says *he* has it, then give it to him. Tell him "Take it!" But keep moving toward the ball anyway. Once in a great while it takes two men to catch a ball. It is always good to have a fielder backing up the guy who tries for the catch. There are no bases to cover in the outfield and the team can afford to have two or even three men rounding up a ball.

Outfielders used to be taught to use two hands on every catch. Nowadays, with the new gloves, even standing catches are made one-handed. But do not try to make catches look hard by slapping at them with the glove and waving the glove behind you. Get that bare hand on the ball so you will be ready to throw in an instant. The bare hand, too, by smothering the ball in the glove, can prevent those high twisting flies from spinning out.

You can usually get into throwing position with a

quick hop to put the foot on the glove side forward. With your weight on your rear foot, you can reach back with your full arm and put all your power into the throw by striding toward the target as you let go.

While center field, even in amateur ball, is the most demanding job in the outfield, right field, among the amateurs and in school baseball, can have some special problems. That is because most batters in school baseball and on the sandlots are right-handed and not all have learned to get around fast on a pitch. So they habitually swing a little late and put many hits into short right field.

Therefore, it is usually good strategy (unless you are up against a right-handed batter you *know* can pull the ball) to play a *very* short right field. Many a humpbacked line drive that usually goes for a hit in this league will drop right into your hands if you are playing up close. And, better than that, sometimes a short straight drive over the first baseman's head will land close enough so you can field it instantly and actually throw the man out at first. Many an amateur batter takes for granted that a line drive over first is good for a single and he will not put on full pressure going for the base. You can surprise him by sneaking halfway in from your position and being ready to field the ball on the first bounce, like an infielder. Once in a great while, of course, you will come up against a right-handed batter who can hit for distance to right field. But on the sandlots the percentage is heavily against such a development. And it does add a lot of merriment to the game to make unexpected outs in the manner I've described.

One final word of warning: Don't ever bluff a throw from the outfield. A smart base runner, already partway down the baseline, will take off as soon as you have completed your bluff and he will get a full second's start while you are cranking up again to throw.

HIT HARD!
RUN HARD!

Everyone, even pitchers, agrees that hitting the ball is the most fun in the game. There seems to be something about whacking a baseball with all your might that satisfies the soul. Not everyone is built to hit baseballs over the outfield fence or bounce them off a distant wall. But everyone can hit the ball *hard*. Even if you lack the mighty shoulder muscles and the powerful wrists of a great slugger, you can still hit a moving baseball sharply and squarely enough to send it back a good deal faster than it was thrown.

Before you learn to hit hard you have to learn to hit in the first place, and that is a job that requires far more practice than you might think. Just playing the game two, three, or four times a week will never provide the practice you need to become really skilled at hitting. If you are devoted enough to baseball to want to play it at the top of your ability, then you will have to set aside a lot of time for learning how to hit.

It really is not necessary to start off by buying a fancy bat with a big-league name on it and finding a place where you have room to drive a baseball a long way. You can practice just as well by swinging a broomstick or a plastic bat and swinging at a tennis ball or a rubber ball or a plastic ball that is built to drop dead after it flies a few feet. Or you can hang a ball on a string somewhere and swing at that. This will at least give you an idea of what it takes to make the bat meet the ball.

Most people will tell you that your first concern should be your stance — that you should find a stance that is comfortable and then stick to that. But you might be comfortable standing right on the plate, or holding the bat drooping at your side. The important thing is to find a way to stand that gives you confidence that you can hit the ball with the bat. You will find you will have a freer swing if you try to keep your elbows away from your body and cock your wrists as you hold the bat high behind your ear. By cocking your wrists, I mean bending them so that the bat is held upright about at your shoulder as you stand with your left side (right side for left-handers) toward the pitcher. But some good batters don't do it that way. They hold the bat in a more relaxed manner and cock the wrists only as they start their batting motion. Doing it first however saves you a little time on the swing and so enables you to be ready a split second sooner.

The actual batting motion begins with a *backward* movement, like the winding of a spring or the drawing back of a bowstring. You pull your bat a little farther behind you, twist your body a little away from the pitcher, and put most of your weight on your back foot.

Then when you see the ball coming to the spot where you want to hit it, you step forward, or shift your weight forward, depending on how widely you have spread your feet in your stance, and bring your bat down and *through* the ball.

Most batting coaches will advise you to get your wrists on a level with the ball and swing a *level* bat right through it. But when the ball comes through the lower part of the strike zone, you simply cannot get your wrists on a level with it, unless you go into a crouch that will immobilize you. You have to lower the fat part of the bat a little and complete your swing that way. I think that if you learn the limits of your own strike zone (over the plate, between knees and shoulders as you stand in natural stance), you will just naturally adjust your bat so that it will meet any ball that comes through there.

Far more than details of technique, you need *confidence*. Confidence is what gives you a nice smooth swing, without any hitches, hesitations, or cramping up. If you just *know* you can hit any ball that comes through that zone, you will begin to swing freely and easily at the ones you like. The first thing to think about is training eyes and muscles to enable you to make contact with the

ball. Start with a ball that is easy to hit, even if you have
to hang it up somewhere to swing at it. Then experiment
with different ways of hitting it *hard*. The idea is not to
poke it, or push it, or stop it, but to *attack* it. Take a good
hard look at it and decide you are going to kill it by
smacking it sharply with the thick part of the bat. While
you will not always be trying to "kill" the ball in the
sense of driving it out of the park, and while your coach
will undoubtedly beseech you just to "meet" the ball
when you start to play for real, you still should want to
hit sharply. If you are not built to drive out home runs,
you can control your bat by cutting down on your swing.
That is, instead of swinging so wildly that you twist
yourself all the way around to complete your natural
follow-through, you swing only partway around. But you
still hold back until the ball is right in front of you
and then you swing sharply, to bring your bat right
through it.

The key to confidence is learning to keep your eye on
the ball. Tell yourself right from the beginning that you
are going to see exactly *where* the bat meets the ball, just
what part of the bat, that is. When ball and bat do meet,
you should be sighting right down the bat — not looking

off into the distance to see where the ball will fall, but staring hard at where ball and bat came together.

You can practice this sighting anywhere, and on the diamond you can get very good practice by standing at the plate while someone pitches and watching the ball *all the way by*, right into the catcher's glove. Just stand there, without swinging. Keep your eye on the ball from the minute you see it in the pitcher's hand to the moment the catcher catches it.

For practice in keeping your eye on the ball, bunting drill is excellent. Bunting is not hitting by any means. Many batters become poor bunters because they never do learn that bunting is not hitting, and they go after the ball instead of letting it come to them. But bunting requires you to keep your eye right on the ball every instant. So, while it will not help your batting swing and will not develop the healthy habit of attacking the ball as it approaches, it can be very helpful in forming the even better habit of seeing the ball all the way in to the plate. It also will develop your confidence in your ability to stand up to any sort of pitching and to stay loose at the plate.

Most players who bunt poorly either fail to bend their

knees to get the bat on a level with the ball, or lunge at the ball, trying to poke it in a certain direction, or just hold on to the bat too tightly. To get your bat on a level with the ball and still be able to sight right over the bat, as you must, you simply have to bend your knees. The proper stance on a sacrifice bunt is facing the pitcher squarely, with the feet side by side, in the front end of the batter's box. Present the bat toward the pitcher, with your elbows slightly bent. You try to keep the bat at about eye level and above all hold it *loosely*. If you grip the bat tightly, you are almost certain to pop the pitch into the air for an easy out, maybe even a double play. But if you hold it loosely, the ball, when your bat meets

it properly, will drop to the ground and roll away from the plate. Just bear in mind that you are not trying to hit the ball in any particular direction. You are just trying to *catch* the ball on the bat. The direction of the roll can be controlled somewhat by the angle of the bat. But if you just catch the ball, drop it to the ground, and let it roll right back toward the pitcher, you are going to have a successful sacrifice nine times out of ten.

You can hold the bat with hands a few inches apart well up on the handle, or you can slide one hand all the way to the label. The exact grip does not matter, so long as it is not tight. The bat must give a little to the ball to keep it from popping into the air.

Bunting to get on base is a different proposition and requires a different move, for you do not want to give away your intent by squaring around to face the pitcher. A drag bunt is usually best worked by a left-hander, who can take a couple of steps toward the ball as it comes in and actually begin to move toward first before he makes contact with the ball. But he must *not* get both feet out of the box before the ball hits the bat or he is out. For this type of bunt, you take your regular batting position. Then, as the pitch comes in, if it is where you want it to be, you lower the bat quickly, sliding your left hand up toward the label, and start to move, with your eye on the ball all the time. The bat should be dead level across the strike zone, on a level with the pitch, and you can carry the bat right into the ball for a step.

A right-hander bunting to get on base just stops his swing by pulling in his left elbow, to bring the bat level across the plate. His body will be turned partway toward the pitcher as he catches the ball on the bat.

It may seem strange to talk about bunting before talking about hitting. But bunting is really valuable to any kind of hitter. Look on it as practice in keeping your eye on the ball and in helping you feel confident at the plate.

When you first start to hit pitched balls, you will be swinging at them. But by that time you should be in the habit of watching them hit the bat (or trying to, because in truth it is almost impossible to see the actual contact) and you should be concerned with attacking only those pitches that come into the strike zone. Do not get into the extremely bad habit of "stopping" bad pitches as a favor to the pitcher or the guy who is retrieving the balls. Let every pitch that is out of the strike zone, no matter how good it looks or how long you have been waiting, go right through to the backstop.

In the beginning you should not be concerned with distance. Try to hit the ball where it is pitched. This way you will hit an outside pitch, if you are right-handed, into right field more often than not, while an inside pitch will go the other way.

One of the best ways to help your club is to learn to hit to right field. A lefty does this naturally by following through vigorously on his swing. A right-hander has to delay his swing a little. But he still does not try to aim the ball. The delay in the swing will send it in the right direction. You still swing right through it as if to stun the thing or squash it flat. Of course an inside pitch is a tough one to hit to right, for a right-hander. But it can be done, if you learn to wait on the pitch. If you can't get the hang of it, and you are supposed to hit to right (with a runner on second, for instance, and none out), then wait for an outside pitch.

To my way of thinking the hit-and-run play, even more than the double play, is a lost cause in amateur baseball. Even in big-league ball there is no oversupply of batters who can hit behind the runner when called upon to do so. All the same, an ability to hit to right is a skill you should try to develop, once you have begun to feel sure of yourself at bat. Then, sometimes, the runner can take off on a steal and you can take a swipe at the ball if it is in the strike zone in hopes of getting him all the way to third.

Your batting stance is something you develop through experimentation. It used to be that old-timers would warn you *never* to change your stance once you had found a comfortable one. That is all right if you are hitting the ball regularly. But what if you are not hitting, or if there are certain pitches in the strike zone that you always miss? You have got to think about changing your stance, right? Well, many fine batters have made changes in their stances to improve their hitting. Rogers Hornsby for instance, after experimenting with different styles, found he did best by standing in the far rear corner of the batter's box, as far away as he could get from the plate. Stan Musial learned to twist himself almost away from the pitcher so he could pull the pitches. Other batters have developed crouches or opened or closed their stances to find the position that gave them the most confidence in their ability to hit all kinds of pitching. Some batters have "opened" their stances completely, so that they are nearly facing the pitcher as the ball comes to the plate. Others have stood with the front foot closer to the plate than the rear foot, so that they are partially turned away from the pitcher.

Some good hitters have used wide stances, and have stepped forward no more than an inch or two as they swung at the ball. Others have held their feet close together and have taken a relatively long stride into the pitch. One thing they all have had in common: When they set out to hit the ball they stepped right into the pitch. Even the men with the "foot in the bucket" — that is, the front foot pointing off toward either first or third base — have moved their front foot *forward*, toward the pitcher, as they swung. This shifting of the weight from rear foot to front foot is the indispensable part of the swing, and it must be *toward* the pitch, and not off toward foul ground.

Men who use the open stance, almost facing the pitcher, do so on the theory that they get a better look at inside pitches that way. Men who use the opposite method, with the front shoulder half turned to the pitcher, seem to feel they can "pull" the ball better — that is, take it from where it is pitched and drive it to the nearest field — left field for a right-hander, right field for a left-hander.

You should adjust your stance depending on your own skills and preference. Take the position that makes you feel most confident of hitting the ball and adjust it to compensate for any weaknesses you may discover. If you are unable to hit outside pitches, try getting closer to the plate, with the front foot closer than the rear foot. If close pitches bother you, move your front foot away from the plate so you can get a good look at the close ones.

I think the distance between your feet is really a matter of comfort. Some hitters lose their concentration if they take too big a stride. Some feel more at ease if they keep their feet close together and even crouch a little. A crouch, if you use it all the time, gives you a smaller strike zone and that may cause the pitcher some trouble. But it also may make it harder for you to learn the strike zone and you may swing at some bad pitches.

Not that it is *always* wrong to swing at bad pitches. There are times when, to help protect a runner, you may want to whiff at the ball. Or perhaps when a pitcher is trying to "pitch around" you to keep you from driving in a runner from second or third, you may have to haul off on a bad pitch to avoid being walked. Helping the team score runs is more important than improving your average.

The one thing you must remember about standing at the plate is that you are up there to hit the ball, not to conform to some standards as to stance and behavior. So any changes you make in your methods should be in the direction of making it easier to hit the ball sharply and frequently. Perhaps at the start you will be influenced by a fear of being hit by the ball and you may make yourself ready to bail out at any moment by sticking your tail out too far, so you are just pecking at the ball with your bat and not getting your hips into the swing. Or you may keep shifting your rear foot from nervousness about being planted too solidly. These are two habits you should try hard to break.

If you keep your eye on the ball at all times, you will be able to drop right on your duff when it is coming at you. You will do this instinctively and you don't need to prepare for a bail-out the moment you get up there. As a matter of fact, in amateur ball, so many pitchers use a sidearm motion for curves that many pitches that *seem* to be coming at you will sweep to the outside of the plate, well away from you. So stand in there and don't jump away until you see the ball is coming for you. Then you just drop into the dirt. Those "brush-back" pitches, as they are politely called, count for you. Four of them and you get a free walk to first.

The pitcher, when you are at bat, is going to be working to make you hit a pitch he feels sure he can get you out on — "his" pitch. And you will be looking for a pitch you feel sure you can hit safely — "your" pitch. Of course there will be some guys who will have nothing in mind but to fire every pitch right past you. But they are not often successful pitchers and, unless they have excellent control, can be made to work for you. At any rate, you should try, through constant practice, to cultivate the confidence that you can hit any pitcher alive if he will just put a pitch into your strike zone. So you need not go fishing wildly after everything the pitcher offers.

When you are up against a new pitcher, take time to look at what he offers. If his first pitch, which will probably be one he has great faith in, misses the strike zone, take a look at another one. There are many professional hitters who will brag that they *never* hit a ball before having at least one strike on them. At any rate, by waiting a new pitcher out a little you may be able to get a line on how fast he is and what sort of curve he has. Then you can decide what you want to hit.

The grip you take on your bat will be a matter of preference and confidence too. But, unless you are going to bunt the ball, it should be a *tight* grip. Really squeeze that bat handle in your hands, or you will not transmit all your power to striking the ball. And be sure your bat suits *you*. Just because a bat has a famous name on it does not mean that it will help you hit like a great slugger. The size and weight of the bat has a great deal to do with your confidence. Pick out a bat that gives you the feeling you can hit *anything* with it. A lot of young batters choose big bats and then choke up on them to get good control. That is a good tactic. But I think it is even better to select a shorter bat, no matter how unstylish it may be, which you are able to swing full length.

When you step up to the plate armed with a weapon you know you can control, your confidence will increase. Just be sure the bat will cover the whole width of the plate so that you will be able to get the fat part of the bat on a ball that cuts across the extreme outside edge of the plate. If it won't reach, perhaps you need to stand a little closer. Or perhaps you do need a longer bat.

Most batters nowadays use bats that would have been considered too light by old-time sluggers. (Babe Ruth used a bat weighing about three pounds.) That is because hitters have learned it pays to be able to move a bat swiftly — to wait until the ball is in range and then whip the bat right through it. But there are still hitters who want a bat that is relatively thick all the way down to the handle, so that no matter what part of the bat they strike the ball with, there will still be enough "good wood" to send the ball flying. My own feeling is that young players probably do best with bats that are somewhat shorter than the average, so that they will be able to hold them level, without strain, as they swing at a pitched ball.

There may be times, even with a shorter bat, when you will want to choke it a little to improve your control, as when you are trying to chop a ball to the ground, against a drawn-in infield, in order to bring a runner in from third. But you will try that sort of thing only when you have developed complete confidence in your ability to put the bat on the ball.

Actually, if you swing a bat that is too heavy for you for a while, your proper weight bat will feel light as a stick. That is why big leaguers put those metal "doughnuts" on their bats as they wait to get up. When they drop the extra weight, the bat feels natural and easy. So it is good sometimes to swing a too-heavy bat in practice, just as a way of developing your wrists and forearms. Then pick up your regular bat and see how easy it is to handle. Of course you will do most of your practice hitting with the size bat that suits you.

If you want to hit really well, you must practice and practice and practice. Get your pitcher to throw you the sort of pitches you have a hard time with. But you also want some pitches that are easy to hit too, because batting practice is of no value if it does not give you a chance to hit, to level off on the ball and savor the enjoyment of smacking it sharply.

When you do hit the ball, unless it is clearly foul, you should take off for first base hard and fast. Run out every ball, no matter if it just rolls back to the pitcher. Baseballs do get stuck in pitcher's gloves sometimes. Throws go wild — with fair frequency in amateur ball — and if you keep the pressure on the defense by running top speed to first, you may cause someone to hurry with his fielding and hurry the throw. Even if you get a walk, *run* to first base, especially if the last pitch is a wild one. The ball is alive on a walk and if it does trickle past the catcher you may catch him completely by surprise and wind up safe at second.

When you run to first, remember to run outside the baseline if the ball is behind you. If you run on the baseline or inside the baseline, the umpire may find you guilty of interfering with the throw and call you out. If it is going to be a close play at first, dig right straight for the bag. You don't have to stop there, so there is no need to slacken speed on your approach. But don't make the mistake of trying to shorten the distance by taking one final long leap. Breaking stride that way will actually slow you down a fraction of a second. Better dig your hardest, in your regular stride.

If your hit has been a long one, you should look for the ball as you approach first base, to see if you have a chance to make second. Often, if the ball has gone to the glove side of the outfielder, he is going to run into a small delay in getting off a throw and you may have a chance for an extra base. Make the decision to try for second before you get to first and start your turn for second then. Tag the base on the *inside corner*. (Do not try to run over the middle of the bag.) Then start straight for second. You don't have to look at your footing as you run down the line. There won't be any wheelbarrows in your way. Look to where the ball is being fielded and see what your chances are of making it to third. If the ball has not yet been picked up, start your turn for third *before* you get to second. Do not wait for the third base coach to wave you on. You have to make up your own mind about trying for third *before* you get to second base. If you wait until you have rounded the base and for the coach to give you the green light, you will have broken stride and may never make it.

Of course you keep your eye on the coach as you head for third. He will tell you if you have to put on the brakes and scramble back. He will signal you with one hand up and the other hand waving you along if you are to stop at third but still make your turn. He will have both hands up if you are not to go any further. And he will put both hands down flat if you are to slide.

In amateur ball, where a high percentage of throws are off target, it is almost always good strategy, when you have a base safely made, to try to draw a throw by making a turn and taking a few steps toward the next base. You should watch the man with the ball and keep bluffing an advance. Scramble back if he throws, but stay alert for an overthrow. If he is smart enough to run right at you, bluffing a throw, the best thing to do is get right back.

Running bases is almost as much fun as hitting, because it offers a chance to be aggressive, to keep the enemy, especially the pitcher, off balance, and to help your club by getting into scoring position. Speed is important in baserunning, but it is not the number one requirement. As a matter of fact, speed can get you into trouble sometimes if you use it blindly and depend on it to get you out of a jam. The successful base runner is the one who is alert for openings, keeps his eye on the ball, can get a good start on the pitcher, knows how to slide, and can control his speed. Controlling your speed means moving down the baseline at a speed suited to the situation — top speed when you are trying to beat a throw, moderate speed when you are watching the outfield, hoping for a chance to proceed but planning to scramble back, and slowly when you are just taking a lead or trying to draw a throw.

You are not really a complete hitter until you know how to run the bases. Only the batters who put the ball over the fence every few times at bat can afford to neglect baserunning. And even *they* have to remember to touch the bases on their way around the diamond.

Touching the bases is something everybody should practice. When you are "rounding" a base, you do not really go around it or even go over it. You tag the inside corner to make the journey as short as possible, and you take a straight path from one base to the next, swinging wide only when you are approaching one base and mean to try for the next.

Sliding is really a simple business, even though it takes some confidence to perform it properly. Sliding was considered a cowardly and childish act in the early days, and the first sliders just sat down suddenly on the base-line and slid in feet first to avoid the tag. Then base runners began to throw themselves headlong into the bases, sliding on their bellies. The old chant used to go: "Slide, Kelly! Slide! Slide, Kelly, on your belly! Slide, Kelly! Slide!" (Kelly was Mike Kelly of Chicago and Boston.)

A head-first slide is still useful nowadays in diving back to a base on an attempted pickoff. But it is a dangerous method to use, particularly in sliding home, where you may bang into a lot of hard armor that the catcher wears. The most useful slide to practice is the pull-up slide, where you actually ride in on your shin, with one leg bent in at right angles and the other out straight. This position enables you to come right to your feet as you complete the slide, in case there is no tag and you want to be ready to draw a throw or move on if there is an error.

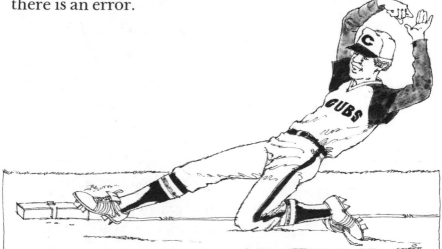

There is no way to learn this slide except by practicing it. One thing you do have to keep in mind is that you must keep your body straight as you ride in, not rolling to one side or the other. If you go to one side, you have a tendency to put one hand on the ground and that can lead to a jammed finger or wrist. Many big-league base runners remind themselves to keep their hands off the ground by picking up handfuls of gravel while they are leading off a base. Then, when they slide, they throw up their hands to get rid of the gravel.

The fall-away or hook slide is the one you use to avoid a tag. What you actually do is slide *away* from the base, on the side opposite the fielder, and trail one foot to

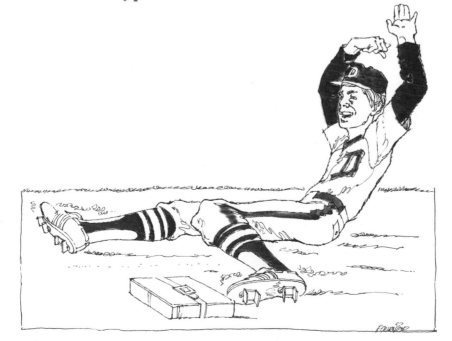

hook the base as you slide past. This time instead of bending your leg inward, you bend it out to provide the "hook." Practicing these slides is actually good fun all by itself, if you can find any kind of sliding pit — just a length of soft earth you can slide in and get your pants nice and dirty in without scraping off any skin.

Just plain running is indispensable exercise for every ballplayer. It keeps your legs strong, builds your stamina, improves your wind, and helps you control your weight. Every chance you get you should run. Every day if you can find room and the weather permits it. (If you can't get out to run, try running up and down a stairs.) But it is best if you can get an opportunity to practice running around bases.

Practice for a hitter of course is hitting. But there are some other exercises you can do that will help your work at the plate. One of the best is hitting a target with a bat. You can hang up an old tire somewhere and mark a white X on it, then stand batting distance away from it and bang it with all your might. You'd be surprised how much fun that is. And it will help not only in sighting down the bat to make sure you hit the target but in strengthening all the muscles you use in hitting. As a boxer adds strength to his punch by hitting a heavy bag, you can put punch into your batting swing by slamming a hard target full strength. Remind yourself as you practice to keep your eye on the target, to step into it as you swing, and to *squeeze* your bat handle hard.

As you warm up before throwing by making a dozen or more easy throws, so you should warm up before batting by engaging in any movement that will get the blood circulating in arms and shoulders and hands. Hitting a ball when your hands are cold can really make them sting and can even sting your forearms too.

If you do not do other rough work, squeezing the bat hard with your hands is going to raise a few blisters to begin with. Eventually they will turn into calluses and make your hands hard. And when your hands are hard you can hit hard.

Many advisers will tell you that you must avoid trying to hit too hard, that you should not think of driving the ball out of the park but should just "meet" the ball with the bat. That is good advice. But it is often misunderstood. When people think of "meeting" an object, they think of running up against it gently, not colliding with it or hammering it. And you do not want to be gentle with a pitched ball. Of course if you try all the time to knock it out of the park, you are going to be thinking too much of strength and distance and too little of the accuracy needed in bringing bat and ball together. You should "meet" a pitched ball the way you "meet" a nail with a hammer — smartly, and right on the nose. If you swing too fiercely, you will be lunging at the ball, spoiling your aim. If you swing too gently, you will not hit the ball squarely or it will get by you untouched. So you swing smartly, with the combined strength of legs, back, shoulders, wrists and hands, and you carry the bat right "through" the ball. If you time this "meeting" just right, the bat will strike the ball when you have all your strength in the swing, and at a place where the bat is about at a right angle to the flight of the ball.

It is this timing that enables you to hit the long ball and it is this timing that the pitcher tries to upset by changing speed on you, trying to get you to step into the pitch too soon, so that you have only your arms in your swing and not the rest of your strength.

There are some aspects of batting and running that you will probably not want to work on until you have a full grasp of the fundamentals. One of these is the chopping "butcher-boy" method of hitting, between a bunt and a swing, that is called the Baltimore chop because it was used many years ago by the original Baltimore Orioles, who liked to bounce the ball on the ground sometimes so the infield could throw it around. And in amateur ball nowadays, where so many throws are off target, that is still a pretty good way of doing business when you desperately need a run.

In the butcher-boy stroke, you do not use a full swing. You choke up well on the bat, shortening your grip almost as you would for a bunt. But you still maintain a tight grip on the bat and you do not square around to face the pitcher. You open your stance a little as the pitch comes in. Then you actually chop down on the ball so that it will bounce high through the infield. If the chop is properly executed, it has a good chance of bouncing high enough to keep the infielders from gloving it before a runner on third, for instance, can cross the plate.

In using the butcher-boy chop or in bunting you should always remember that you should try it only when the pitch is in the strike zone. Unless the suicide squeeze has been called for, you do not need to make an effort to hit balls that you have to reach out of the strike zone to hit.

In the big leagues, even sacrifice bunters do not always square around to face the pitcher. Instead they just move the rear foot a little closer to the plate as the pitch comes in and drop the bat to a blocking position right across the plate on a level with the pitch. They also hold the bat a little more tightly, but with the arms still relaxed enough so that they will give with the pitch. This gives them better control of the bat so they can angle it to send the ball in any direction they choose. But the chance of fouling-off the ball or popping it up are greatly increased by this maneuver and I don't think it is necessary in amateur ball, where you seldom have to fear that a double play will grow out of a sacrifice.

When you have two strikes on you, you must be careful to guard the plate. Old-time coaches used to tell batters in these circumstances: "Never trust the umpire!" What they meant was that you should not assume that because a ball looks to you as if it is just out of the strike zone, the umpire will agree. So, when you are in a hole this way, you must be ready to guard the plate by swinging at any pitch that looks close to the strike zone. Don't go after real bad ones. But don't pass up the near-misses.

Another good two-strike stunt that you can use when you have confidence in your speed and your eye is to swing at a really wild pitch — one that hits the dirt or is going far over your head. A swing and a miss in that situation (unless first base is occupied or there are two out) means you can try for first. And if the ball is going past the catcher, you have a good chance of making it. But don't try it unless you can really *run*.

Good ballplayers start to hit before they get up to the plate. That is, while they are waiting in the on-deck circle they time the pitcher, perhaps even swinging the bat as the pitch comes to the plate, to get into the rhythm. They will be going over the coach's signs in their minds. If they are mixed up about any or have forgotten any, they will go talk to the coach before they take their position at the plate. They will try to figure what they might be asked to do if the man now hitting gets on base. Will they have to bunt him to second? If he hits for two bases, will they have to hit to right to move him over? Will he be stealing? Get some of these possibilities clear in your mind before you get up and you will be able to concentrate better on your job at the plate. It goes without saying that you should know before you get up, before you even go to the on-deck circle, what the score is, what inning it is, and how many are out. Keep asking yourself these questions all the time you are on the bench and be sure you know the answers. I have seen even big leaguers walk into easy put-outs because they thought the third out had already been made.

At the plate, concentrate on the ball. Don't let the catcher distract you with questions, comments, or wise-cracks. Watch the ball from the very moment the pitcher takes his position and don't take your eye from it until it hits the bat or lands in the catcher's glove. But between pitches, be sure to take a look at the coach. Is he giving you a sign? If he is, don't look away at once. Keep looking, so you won't give the sign away. But if you don't understand the sign, step right out of the box and go find out what's wanted. There's no law against that.

When you get on base, you have to know at all times just where the ball is. Did the baseman really give it back to the pitcher? Don't leave the base until you know. Watch the pitcher. He is not allowed to take his position on the mound without the ball. Is he hesitating about getting into pitching position? Maybe he is waiting for the infielder to put the tag on you. Stay put with your foot on the base until you know for sure.

The standard lead off first is the length of your body, plus one stride. The theory is that, if the pitcher starts to throw over to first, you will just have time to turn and dive back headlong. If you have no skill at such maneuvers, take less ground. Go just as far as you know you can go and still beat the throw back to base. It may take some practice to learn how far that is.

If you are planning to steal, you must keep close watch on the pitcher. It is best if you have been studying him in action in the game and know if there are any giveaway signs to show when he is going to throw to the plate. Not many amateur pitchers have had time to perfect their moves on the mound and many of them reveal their intentions plainly. Perhaps one pitcher will bring his elbows in tight to his side just before he is *really* going to pitch. Perhaps another may shift the position of his rear foot only when he is going to the plate. Maybe one will even duck his head a little as he starts his pitching move. Learning signals like this will give you a real head start on a steal and will make your success almost certain.

But if the pitcher does not give himself away, you should wait until you *know* he is going to pitch the ball and not throw it to first. One way to be sure is to watch the heel of his rear foot. When you see daylight under that, you can be pretty sure he is pitching.

Some people will tell you to start a steal by first moving the foot nearest second base and avoiding a crossover step. I don't think it makes much difference. Start in a natural way — with a quick shove and a crossover step or with a move by the right foot first, whichever suits you. Then dig for the base. Watch the infielder who covers. He will tell you by his position on which side the ball is coming and you can slide away from him. Or if he straddles the bag, you can use a pull-up slide, to be ready to keep going if the throw gets by him.

In leading off second base, you have to concern yourself mostly with the position of the shortstop. You will be able to see the second baseman and can get back to the base if he starts for it. But the shortstop will be out of your vision most of the time and you should take a quick glance now and then to make sure he is not closer to the base than you are. If he is, shorten your lead so he will not be able to beat you back to the bag. Many runners have always felt that it was easier to steal third base than to steal second. But it also is easier to get picked off at second base, because the pitcher can make any kind of move he wants to second without danger of a balk being called. Also, with two infielders to work on you, there is that "daylight" or "count" play that can catch you unaware. That is why you must take extra care to make sure the shortstop does not get closer to the bag than you are.

It is true that often, with a man on second base, the defense is concentrating so on the batter that you can sometimes get a nice long lead, particularly if the short-stop plays deep in the hole. But if you are not quick on your feet, better be satisfied with a conservative lead. A runner on second is too valuable to his team to take long chances. But you should be aggressive all the same. Always move up a few steps on the pitch, ready to go if the ball is hit. Keep your eye on the catcher and if the ball goes by the batter, shorten your lead quickly.

If the ball is hit ahead of you, be sure it has gone through before you get too far from the base. You don't want to run into a put-out. That does not mean you should just stay put if the ball goes in front of you.

Maybe it will have pulled the third baseman far off base and tangled up the shortstop too. Stay alert and grab the base if no one is covering.

On third base, you can take a lead equal to the distance the third baseman plays off the base. And here again you move up on the pitch and shorten up when you see the third baseman approach the bag. A runner on third can often help his club with a convincing bluff on an infield ground ball. If you will put your head down and dig hard for two or three steps you may cause the player who fielded the ball to hesitate about throwing to first, or even to bang the ball home. But you have to be sure you don't outsmart yourself. You have to put the brakes on fast and be ready to scramble back. Don't get so far down the line that you can't recover the base.

The runner on third also has to use his head about scoring on a sacrifice fly. You can't depend entirely on the coach to give you the GO signal, because that will cause you to lose a step that may be crucial. You have to be moving the moment the ball makes contact with the outfielder. But if you play it right, you can actually start moving *before* the ball makes contact. If you will take a position just behind third base with one foot on the base as the ball is in the air you can make your first step with your back foot just before the ball touches the fielder, leaving the other foot on the base as you start. Then you will be actually moving when the catch is made, and can get a flying start.

Remember too, when you are on third base, to take your lead in foul ground. Do not run on the baseline or you are in danger of being put out by being hit by a fair-batted ball. You can *return* to the base in fair territory, for the rules do not require you to leave that open for a throw.

The man on third is the head man on a double steal and has to keep his eyes open to avoid being caught on a bluff throw by the catcher. Have a good lead and be ready to go when the catcher throws to second base. But be sure he *does* throw before you take off. Otherwise you are a dead duck. If you do get caught in a rundown on a delayed steal, or any time there is another runner on base, keep dodging and bluffing as long as you can, to give the other runner a chance to take all the bases he can make.

On any other base, when there is a long fly to the outfield, you can take off when the ball is hit. But go only halfway (unless the ball is obviously going to hit the fence). Then watch to see what happens. If the ball seems certain to be caught, scramble back and tag up, ready to advance if the throw does not go to the base ahead of you. If you are on second base, with one out, and the caught fly will make it two out, getting over to third is not worth the risk. It is still going to take a safe hit (or a wild pitch) to score you.

No base runner should ever get himself doubled on a caught line drive or a pop bunt. Never run blindly on any such play. Look to be sure the ball has hit the ground. As you dig for second base on a sacrifice bunt, it is easy enough to glance back at the plate and make sure the ball is on the ground. You can't count on the coaches to tell you. Use your own head on these plays and be ready to scramble for safety if things go wrong.

There is a fancy type of steal that I think may work better in amateur ball than it would in the major leagues. That is the delayed steal, the one you make after the ball has gone by the batter. Say you are on first base and have moved up several steps with the pitch. Everybody on the defense has his eyes centered on the plate. The catcher gloves the ball and does not even glance your way. The second baseman and shortstop are both well off the bag. You take off! You have a good fat lead already and the catcher is going to have to make a hurried throw to get you — and has to wait until there is someone to take the throw. This does not work with a really alert catcher and infield. But if you notice that the catcher is not checking your lead as he should after every pitch, this is a good aggressive play that will throw the defense into confusion.

A lot of amateur base runners get so involved in their own speed and readiness to take extra bases that they sometimes forget there may be a runner ahead. Of course the coaches on the baselines will be trying hard to remind you. But you take note always of just where other runners are. If you do ever wind up on the same base as another runner, remember that the base belongs to the guy who got there first and it is up to you to get back to the previous base alive.

And all the time you are on base, stay awake to where other players are. Don't take a long lead off second base without knowing exactly where the infielders are. A short lead with a good start is better than a long lead on which you have to wait and look around before you dare take off.

EQUIPMENT

Amateur players should not fret over not owning the choicest equipment. High-priced caps and heavy flannel pants and stirrup stockings are not essential. But there are a few things you should not be without. I think the first thing you should spend money on and take good care of should be your shoes. Loose spikes on your shoes can do you a serious injury. They can twist a pitcher's ankle or cause him to lose his footing. They can make a catcher stumble over the plate, can send an infielder on his ear, or even sprain an ankle in the outfield.

So look to those shoes first of all. If you can't get a good set of spikes you'd better play in sneakers. Ideally you should have two pairs of baseball shoes — one to practice in, to get them broken in, and one to play regular games in. Baseball shoes will stretch a good deal from wear, so it is best to get them a little small and break them in slowly. Otherwise they may begin to flop on your feet after a few weeks.

Next should be your glove. The pitcher above all should own the biggest glove he can get his hand into — not just for concealing the ball from the batter, but to fling up in front of his face if a line drive should come straight back at him. The finger part of the glove, which is really a scoop these days, should be relatively stiff so it will slow down a line drive. The other players should take care not to try to use gloves that are too big for their hands. Get a glove that you can sling around without having it drop off and that you can wield as if it was part of your body.

I think the break-rim glove that can be folded over the ball is best for today's one-handed catching behind the plate. Don't get one so stiff that pitches will bounce off it. And don't ever buy one of those manhole-cover things (if they still make them) that some catchers used for catching knuckleballs. They just don't work. Better to deal with a knuckleball by trying to snatch it out of the air at the last second. You won't miss any *more* that way, and you'll be able to handle the ones you do catch.

A good sweat shirt is a necessity for a pitcher and he

should plan on using two a day when he pitches. Taking off a soaking sweat shirt in the middle of the game and pulling on a dry one is like shedding five pounds, or like getting your second wind. Sweat socks are of course a necessity. Some players like to wear a thin pair of under-socks and another pair over them, then the stirrup socks to cover the leg. That seems to cut down on blisters but I think that system works better with basketball shoes than with baseball shoes.

The players who catch a lot of throws — infielders and catchers — almost always will keep one finger outside the glove to ease the pounding on the first joints that they get from today's gloves. And many catchers use that extra padding that some girls wear — only the guys use it inside the glove to soften the impact when they have a fireballer pitching.

Infielders and outfielders should all have flip-down sunglasses if the budget will stand it. They do make a lot of catches possible on sunny days, especially in the late summer when the sun seems to shine straight into your eyes so often. Batting gloves are nice too in avoiding the blisters that come from squeezing the bat the way you should. Actually they are good to have on the bases if you get careless about putting your hands up when you slide straight in. But I don't think they are a necessity like sunglasses.

Most schools and amateur leagues will see to it that you wear head protection when you are at the plate. It helps give you confidence, especially against sidearm pitching. And I think batting helmets are useful on the bases too, to protect from wild throws.

SIGNS AND SIGNALS

Every club needs signals of some sort, if only so that the catcher will know what to expect from the pitcher. There is no need for the catcher's signals to be complicated. Nearly everyone uses the same signals, and as long as the catcher keeps them concealed, no one is going to steal them. It is standard to show one finger for fast ball and two for curve. (The curve ball is known everywhere as "number two.") I think it just as well not to have a three-finger sign, because it can be confusing at a distance. Just showing the index finger and the little finger can be a third sign, if any is needed. And a change-up can be signaled for with four fingers or a closed fist.

Catchers should also indicate where the pitch should go, by rubbing one knee or the other with the bare hand and by simply pointing thumb or finger up or down for

high or low. A pickoff (at second base) can be signaled for by picking up a bit of dirt.

The signs for the batter and base runners are best given by the third base coach, because everyone can see him without turning around, except the runner on third base, whom he can talk to. His signs too should be simple, and controlled by an "on" sign and an "off" sign. And these should be as easy to remember as possible. As a matter of fact, the same three signs can be used all the time, with their meaning changed after a certain inning. Thus a hand touching bare flesh (cheek or fore-arm) can mean "take this pitch," a hand brushing cloth above the waist can mean "bunt" and a hand brushing cloth below the waist can mean "steal" — for the first five innings. Then for the rest of the game, the meanings can be reversed. And the signals can be concealed by having them mean nothing unless the "on" sign is given. For instance, all signals may be meaningless if the coach is standing with both feet in the box. And the signal may count if the coach has one foot out of the box. An "off" sign — meaning "disregard the last sign" — can be given by just lifting the cap. Actually signs do not have to be concealed with such care at all times, nor do you always need to signal the batter whether to take a ball or not. I think amateur hitters should go to the plate hitting and can be told to wait a pitcher out by being called out of the box and spoken to. The bunt and the steal signs are important. And a separate sign should be used for the squeeze play which is often so valuable in amateur ball, where hits are scarce. That sign can be a very plain one, like a pounding of fist into the hand, or calling the runner by name: "Heads up, Jones!"

Signals by voice can be exchanged between fielders

now and then, either to warn a third baseman of an inside pitch or to get the second baseman or shortstop to move for the base with the pitch. What outfielders have to say to each other can be said loud and clear. It may be good for the shortstop to have some method of passing the catcher's signs to the outfield so they can be ready to move one way or another. But I think that stuff is superfluous and confusing in most amateur ball.

The one thing you must be sure of is that you have all the signs straight and that the rest of the team has the same idea you have. If there is ever the slightest doubt in your mind on that score, you should ask for time out (only the umpire can "call" time) and make certain you have everything straight.

TACTICS

I am a great believer in suiting the tactics of play to the quality of the league you are playing in. Small schools and amateur nines do not often boast a whole lineup of hitters and many of them have only one or two pitchers who really know their jobs thoroughly. Catchers who can throw hard and fast to second base are not in large supply either. So you should make it part of your job to take a good look at the other club in pre-game practice.

Does the pitcher have a smooth and stylish delivery? Or does he have certain nervous moves or gestures that may give away his intentions? When Babe Ruth first came into the American League as a pitcher, he had a habit of sticking the tip of his tongue out of the corner of his mouth as he worked the ball into his hand for the curve. You can imagine how long it took for the rest of the league to notice *that* and get fat on it!

Maybe your opponent will lift his hands only partway when he throws a curve and all the way over his head if he throws a fast ball. Maybe he will look down into his glove to study his grip as he gets ready for the curve. Maybe he will hunch his shoulders before every pitch.

Watch the catcher especially. Can he throw a straight hard throw to second base without running partway to the mound? Or do his throws come in slow, humpbacked fashion? If you are up against a catcher like that, you should decide that *everybody* who gets on first should try to steal right away. And if the pitcher gives away his move to the plate, you can figure every single is as good as a two-bagger.

Is the third baseman in the habit of playing flat-footed, well behind the baseline? Then you should feed him one bunt after another, until he learns better.

There is usually at least one arm in the outfield that is not equal to throwing the ball hard, back to the diamond. Watch and see which one it is, and remember in the game that if the ball goes to him while you are on base you have a good chance of making it home from third base after a fly, or from second to third if he is the right fielder.

It is, as I said, good practice in amateur ball to draw throws, because so many throws do go astray. And a hit that must be picked up and thrown quickly, while it may not improve your batting average, may very well, in this league, give you the base on an error.

Bunts are a much-neglected weapon in amateur ball. Yet they are often deadly, just because they require some hurried and successful fielding. If the other pitcher has got your hitters handcuffed, then perhaps you can make some hay by beginning to lay the ball down for him to chase after. It is far easier to learn to bunt than it is to learn to hit, and bunts are often much harder to field than simple ground balls. They almost always require a hurried throw, if your runners have any speed at all.

Surprise bunts, in defiance of all sound strategy, will sometimes succeed beautifully. I saw a school championship won one day by a squeeze bunt with *two out* and two strikes on the batter. The opposition was so upset by the move that *nobody* picked the ball up until the run had scored and the bunter had reached first. That is a one-in-a-thousand stunt, but it gives you an idea of what can be done by taking advantage of the other side's failure to stay on their toes.

It is also possible to score *two* runs on a squeeze play, if the pitcher will just oblige by forgetting the runner at second base and the infield does not remind him. Seeing the batter square to bunt with a man on third sometimes draws *everybody* in over the baseline. And if the runner at second has been able to hold on to the lead he took after the last pitch (no one is worrying about his stealing third with a runner already there) he can dig — not just for third, but for *home* as soon as the pitcher delivers the pitch. Rounding third at full tilt, he can go partway down the baseline and, if the player who fields the bunt throws to first, he can just keep on going. Of course this will not work if the third baseman has been alert enough to stay away from the bunt and cover the base. But often both the third baseman and the pitcher are concentrating on the bunt.

There are many other stunts you can devise to take advantage of weaknesses you may have noticed. And there is great enjoyment in getting away with one of these unorthodox moves.

The real fun of the game, however, will always lie in good hard batting, hard throwing and hard running. Work to build your confidence at the plate, take an aggressive attitude when you are up there, and attack any ball that comes into your strike zone and looks good to you. When you throw the ball, from base to base, from mound to home, from catcher to baseman, or even to pitcher, throw hard. When it is time to run, and the road is clear — run *hard* and slide hard and be ready to advance as soon as the opposition's guard is down. Then, whether you win the game or lose it, you will savor the deep satisfaction of having done your very best, of having turned on your strength and speed to the very limit of your supply.

"Well," you can tell yourself, whatever the outcome, "I gave it all I've got and it was a great ball game!"

About the Author

Robert Smith, editor and compiler of the official playing guides put out by the Major League Baseball Players Association, has written, besides a number of bestselling sports histories, about a dozen "how to play" books in collaboration with many of the top pitchers, catchers, hitters, and managers in the big leagues. In preparing his books, he has gone out on the diamond with the stars, donned a glove, and had them demonstrate in action all the moves they told about. By working with and listening to the stars on the diamond, on the bench, and in the locker room, and in coaching and managing semi-pro and prep school teams, Bob Smith has picked up many of the secrets and the shortcuts and the pet plays that make the game of baseball continually exciting. Most of those he offers in this book in addition to setting forth his own theory that baseball is fun — even if you lose the game; that nice guys often finish first; and that losers give as much to the game and get as much out of it as the winners do.

In short, he says, "Baseball was invented for everybody to enjoy!"